youth ministry BASICS

Authors

Brad Alles

Steve Arnold

Lee A. Belmas

Mary Clark

Tom Couser

Terry K. Dittmer

Audrey Duensing-Werner

Carl Eliason

Peter Hiller

Jerald Joersz

Tim Lindeman

Bob McKinney

Jeffrey E. Meinz

Dave Rahberg

Paul Schoepp

Sue Steege

and Doug Widger

Editors

Mark Sengele

Jane Fryar

CONCORDIA PUBLISHING HOUSE · SAINT LOUIS

Your comments and suggestions concerning these materials are appreciated. Please write the Editor of Youth Materials, Concordia Publishing House, 3558 S. Jefferson Avenue, St. Louis, MO 63118-3968.

This publication may be available in braille, in large print, or on cassette tape for the visually impaired. Please allow 8 to 12 weeks for delivery. Write to the Library for the Blind, 1333 S. Kirkwood Rd., St. Louis, MO 63122-7295; call 1-800-433-3954, ext. 1322; or e-mail to blind.library@lcms.org.

Cover design by Richard Heroldt. Interior design by Karol Bergdolt.

Scripture quotations are taken from the HOLY BIBLE. NEW INTERNATIONAL VERSION®. NIV®. Copyright © 1973, 1978, 1984 by International Bible Society. Used by permission of Zondervan Publishing House. All rights reserved.

"Leading Youth Bible Study" adapted from What I've Learned about Youth Bible Study from BYS Monograph by Tom Couser, © 1995 Youth Ministry—LCMS. Used with permission.

Quotes from Luther's Large Catechism and the Augsburg Confession are reprinted by permission from the Book of Concord, edited by Robert Kolb and Timothy J. Wengert, © 2000 Augsburg Fortress.

Quotes from Augsburg Today, © 1997 Concordia Publishing House. Used by permission.

Quotes from The Proper Distinction between Law and Gospel by C. F. W. Walther, © 1986 Concordia Publishing House. Used by permission.

Quotes from An Asset Builder's Guide to Youth Leadership, © 1999 Search Institute. Used by permission. www.search-institute.org

1   2   3   4   5   6   7   8   9   10   11   10   09   08   07   06   05   04   03   02

Introduction

What is this resource about?

Youth ministry is a dynamic, vital part of the church. The vast majority of those who work with youth are not professional church workers, but volunteers. You may be a church professional, or perhaps you are one of those countless volunteers who bless the church with your service. Whatever your role, you have looked to this resource to assist you in better ministering to an important sector of the church's population.

Almost twenty years ago Concordia Publishing House and the Board for Youth Services of The Lutheran Church—Missouri Synod joined forces to develop a training resource for youth leaders. That resource, called *Lead On*, made use of a set of twelve monographs written by experts in youth ministry. The monographs were designed to be used separately or together as a thorough study of youth ministry.

It is in the spirit of *Lead On* that we have developed *Youth Ministry Basics*. Each of the fifteen chapters in this resource focuses on one particular aspect of youth ministry. While chapters may be studied individually, viewed together they provide a comprehensive study of youth ministry in the church today. Suggestions for an approach to such a comprehensive study follow.

Who are the authors of this resource?

Each of the authors of *Youth Ministry Basics* has a passion for working with youth. Like the writers in *Lead On*, the authors' particular interest or focus in ministry is reflected in the subject of the chapter. The authors include full-time youth leaders, camp directors, and district or national church officials. The authors' professional experiences include leading as pastors, teachers, and directors of Christian education. Through their writing, the authors share their personal passion for the Gospel of Jesus Christ as well as their desire to serve the youth of the church.

How do I use this resource?

In an ideal situation, users of this resource will be able to work through all of the chapters in *Youth Ministry Basics* with other adult leaders. Professional church workers may desire to use *Youth Ministry Basics* to train the volunteer youth leaders in their congregations. In any case, it will be most helpful if each participant has his or her own copy of the book. For situations where this is not possible or when you wish only to review selected lessons, reproducible resource pages are provided with most lessons. Copy and distribute them as indicated in the chapter.

Possible models for study of this resource include the following:

Individual/Small Group Study Model: Each participant works through a chapter or chapters from the book and completes the questions/review activities. Then participants meet to discuss their learning and insights. This model may be used for all of the leaders within a single congregation or perhaps include individuals from one or more neighboring churches. The sharing time may occur weekly, monthly, or quarterly as each participant's schedule allows.

Leadership Training Model: A designated leader (professional church worker) facilitates a series of training sessions using the material from the book for all of the volunteer youth leaders within the congregation. Each month/quarter a chapter or chapters are assigned for study, and the group comes together to discuss their findings. The time together may include an opening devotion, a review of the assigned section along with feedback, a time for discussion and planning of programming for the congregation, and a closing activity. Allow at least one-and-a-half to two hours for each session.

Workshop Training Model: This model may be used within a single congregation or as a circuit/regional training activity. Participants work through selected chapters from Youth Ministry Basics *under the direction of one or more leaders. The day-long session is designed to focus on two or more chapters. Most groups choose to begin with a review of the lessons on Word and Sacraments and developing a philosophy of youth ministry. If a number of churches are participating, the leaders may wish to consider establishing a series of training sessions that rotate from church to church.*

The Foundation of Youth Ministry: Word and Sacrament

BY JERALD JOERSZ

The Miracle of Sight and Sound

Sound waves reverberating and striking the tympanic membrane of the ear . . .

Can it be that through this miracle of creation, another, more wondrous, act of God takes place? Is it possible that "in, with, and under" the sound waves, the Word of the eternal God Himself comes to us? Is it really possible that "in, with, and under" the audible attached to the visible, the Word of the eternal God Himself comes to us?

With adoration and awe, we Christians are eager to respond, "Yes, this is how God comes to us!" The "mystery, which for ages past was kept hidden in God, who created all things . . . has now been revealed by the Spirit to God's holy apostles and prophets." This "mystery," revealed through the Scriptures, is the Gospel of the "unsearchable riches of Christ," through which God's plan to save the world has been accomplished (Ephesians 3:3–13)! This Gospel comes to us through sound and sight: the spoken Word preached and taught, and the visible Word of the Sacraments administered and received (Baptism and the Lord's Supper).

These audible and visible ways of God's entry into our lives are called the "means of grace." They are the instruments—and the only instruments—through which God has promised to communicate and give to us His saving grace revealed in Jesus Christ.

A Voice from Heaven

When we *hear* the Word of the Gospel, it is as if we have heard "God's voice from heaven" (Augsburg Confession, 25, 4). "My sheep hear My *voice*," Jesus said (John 10:27). And when we *see* the water of Baptism and the bread and wine of the Lord's Supper used according to God's command and promise—earthly things to which the Word of forgiveness is attached—God is telling us something. Jesus continues to speak to us through "sight and sound."

Now, the question is, what do we hear when "the voice of the Gospel" comes from God? In our technological age, we might imagine that God has left us a "voice mail" message, so to speak. We are eager to hear the message, and *what* is the message?

"God was reconciling the world to Himself in Christ, not counting men's sins against them." This is *the* message cherished by Christians and committed to them so they can say to themselves, to each other, and to their friends and neighbors, "We implore you on Christ's behalf: Be reconciled to God" (2 Corinthians 5:19–20). Paul therefore calls the Gospel *"the message of reconciliation."* God reconciles people to Himself now through the message of the Gospel.

Without God's reconciling act in history 2,000 years ago in the suffering, death, and resurrection of Jesus Christ, there would, of course, be no need to speak of "Word and Sacraments," the means of grace. Without the historical fact that all sinners "are justified freely by His grace through the redemption that came by Jesus Christ" (Romans 3:24), we would have only "the sounds of silence." No sound waves from heaven, just a message-less "beep." Consequently and sadly, there would be no saving grace revealed to us and we would remain in our sins, without the Holy Spirit, and without faith in Christ.

In his explanation to the Third Article of the Apostles' Creed, Martin Luther put it this way:

Neither you nor I could ever know anything of Christ, or believe in Him and take Him as our Lord, unless these were first offered to us and bestowed on our hearts through the preaching of the Gospel by the Holy Spirit. The work is finished and completed, Christ has acquired and won the treasure for us by His sufferings, death, and resurrection, etc. But if the work remained hidden and no one knew of it, it would have been all

7

in vain, all lost. In order that this treasure might not be buried, but put to use and enjoyed, God caused the Word to be published and proclaimed, in which He has given the Holy Spirit to offer and apply to us this treasure of salvation. (Large Catechism, 2, 38)

Thank God for the ways He has given us to beam His love into our hearts—the Word and the Sacraments!

Ransom in Our Mouths

Jesus said during His Last Supper, "This is My body given for you" and "This is My blood, shed for you." With the words "for you" Jesus "meant to remind [His disciples] that they ought to break forth with joy and gladness because the ransom that was to be paid for the sins of the whole world was, so to speak, *put in their mouths*" (C. F. W. Walther, *The Proper Distinction between Law and Gospel*, 152).

To many, such graphic language may sound offensive. It just does not seem possible that God would take ordinary created things such as sound waves, water, bread, and wine and actually use them to offer and convey to human beings His gifts: the forgiveness of sins, life, and salvation. Yet this is exactly what God our heavenly Father, who sent His only Son into the flesh, has done and continues to do! The Word and Sacraments really give what they announce or proclaim.

The Gospel (the Spoken Word)

St. Paul writes, "I am not ashamed of the gospel, because it is the power of God for the salvation of everyone who believes" (Romans 1:16). For the apostle Peter, too, the Gospel has power: "For you have been born again, not of perishable seed, but of imperishable, through the living and enduring word of God . . . and this is the word that was preached to you" (1 Peter 1:23, 25).

Jesus told His disciples before leaving them that "repentance and the forgiveness of sins will be preached in His name to all nations" (Luke 24:47). When we believe in Christ, we have what He gives (Ephesians 1:7, 13). Literally, the Gospel "talks" forgiveness, life, and salvation into our hearts. The words of Jesus to the paralytic are spoken also to us and are "music to our ears": "Take heart, son [daughter]; your sins are forgiven" (Matthew 9:2).

The miracle continues to happen: the words of Absolution, spoken by pastors and Christians to one another, bring forgiveness to penitent sinners.

Baptism

"God reaches down into the ordinary, takes water and enwraps it with His

Word of command and promise. Just as God entered human flesh in Jesus Christ, who 'lived for a while among us' (John 1:14), so God takes simple water and through His Word becomes present in it" (Jerald Joersz, *Augsburg Today,* 56). With the Word, the water of Baptism becomes a "water of life."

How can this be? How can water do such a great thing? The water of Baptism is such a treasure because it is God's way of conveying His salvation to us: "He saved us through the washing of rebirth and renewal by the Holy Spirit whom He poured out on us generously through Jesus Christ our Savior, so that having been justified by His grace, we might become heirs having the hope of eternal life" (Titus 3:5–7).

The Lord's Supper

"Here in the sacrament you receive from Christ's lips forgiveness of sins, which contains and conveys God's grace and Spirit with all His gifts, protection, defense, and power against death and the devil and all evils" (Large Catechism, 5, 70). What powerful words our Lord Jesus spoke over the bread and wine of the Sacrament: "Given and shed for you for the forgiveness of sins"!

We must remember that each celebration of the Sacrament is an audio/visual event. As the sound waves of the Gospel strike our ears and enter our hearts, so also the consecrating, distributing, and receiving of the bread and wine (body and blood) "enters through the eyes to move the heart" (Large Catechism, 4, 30).

"To Obtain Such Faith"

Technology has literally changed the course of human events. A universe of ideas is rapidly becoming accessible through tiny instruments held in the palms of our hands. Paradoxically, the larger the universe of information, the smaller the devices we use to access it. We stand in awe.

However, the miracle worked by the Word proclaimed and the Sacraments received infinitely surpasses anything human beings can either accomplish or comprehend. Through the message of Christ, by which faith in Him is born, God rescues "us from the dominion of darkness" and brings "us into the kingdom of the Son He loves, in whom we have redemption, the forgiveness of sins" (Colossians 1:13–14).

"Baptism now saves you" (1 Peter 3:21), as the Holy Spirit creates the faith that grasps the grace of God revealed in Christ's saving death and resurrection. The Lord's Supper strengthens that faith by confirming and imparting the benefits of Christ's sacrificial death to those who come to Him.

Through the message of Jesus Christ, God gives His Holy Spirit, who creates faith in the heart. As St. Paul puts it in a well-known passage, "Consequently, faith comes from hearing the message, and the message is heard through the Word of Christ" (Romans 10:17). Jesus prayed for those who would believe through the Word proclaimed by His disciples (John 17:20).

the foundation of youth ministry: word and sacrament

Basics

To obtain justifying faith, confessed our Lutheran fathers, God provided the ministry of the Gospel and the Sacraments: "Through these, as through means, He gives the Holy Spirit, who works faith, when and where He pleases, in those who hear the Gospel" (Augsburg Confession, 5, 1–2).

Paradoxically, the Word and Sacraments, by the power of God's Holy Spirit, create the faith that receives the blessings they offer!

Creating Space for the Word of Christ

Millions of homes in which young people live have created space to capture the sights and sounds of the world and culture around us. Big-screen TVs, digital surround-sound, and the computer monitor have in a sense become symbols of how we arrange our lives to receive and send messages. These messages inform, entertain, inspire, terrify, prompt, captivate, sadden, thrill. . . . In numerous ways our lives are being enriched and enhanced, but they can also be impoverished and deprived. The Word of the eternal and living God can be crowded out, squeezed into a very small corner of life.

"Give space to the Word of Christ," the apostle Paul writes to the Colossians and to us: "Let the word of Christ dwell in you richly as you teach and admonish one another with all wisdom, and as you sing psalms, hymns, and spiritual songs with gratitude in your hearts to God. And whatever you do, whether in word or deed, do it all in the name of the Lord Jesus, giving thanks to God the Father through Him" (3:16–17).

We give space to the Word of Christ by *using* the Word and Sacraments. Christians use the means of grace when they gather as a congregation for public worship. The Word is preached, the Sacraments are celebrated, the people of God listen and learn, and they respond through the "acts" of worship (Adoration, Confession, Thanksgiving, and Supplication). But God calls Christians also in their personal and daily lives to "let the Word of Christ dwell" in them "richly." In "whatever you do, whether in word or deed," implies that the Word of Christ is to permeate our existence here on earth.

A continuing challenge lies before youth leaders, parents, pastors, and the Christian congregation today: to encourage and help the young Christians in their midst to really make use of the "one thing needful," the living and enduring Word of Jesus Christ. Since God awakens and strengthens faith only through the means of grace, every aspect of our ministry to youth needs to be driven by our desire to let the Word of Christ dwell in and among them richly!

"They devoted themselves to the apostles' teaching and to the fellowship, to the breaking of bread and to prayer." Acts 2:42

"Living and Active . . . "

"The Word of God is living and active," says the writer to the Hebrews (4:12). The Gospel in Word and Sacraments is full of energy. When the Spirit of God works through it, things happen. In a sense, youth ministry is a means of the means of grace.

Use Resource Page 1 to analyze, energize, and strategize for youth ministry in your congregation. Try to be as focused as possible as you evaluate the present and envision the future for youth ministry in your congregation. Do all of this personally (in the first person), before you share with others in your group. As you conclude your session, provide adequate time for sharing and summarizing your common hopes and commitments for enabling the Word of Christ to dwell richly among you and your young people.

Resources

Kolb, Robert. *Christian Faith: A Lutheran Exposition* (Concordia Publishing House: 1993).

Mahsman, David. L., ed. *Augsburg Today: This We Believe, Teach, and Confess* (Concordia Publishing House: 1997).

Preus, Robert. *Getting into the Theology of Concord: A Study of the Book of Concord* (Concordia Publishing House: 1977).

Sasse, Herman. *We Confess the Sacraments* (Concordia Publishing House: 1995).

"As I *analyze* what we are doing in youth ministry, this is what I see . . ."

"*To energize* our youth ministry, I think we need to . . ."

"As we *strategize* for youth ministry, here's what we can do . . ."

Teens and Spirituality

BY BRAD ALLES

A Word of Introduction

As you begin this chapter, let me clarify one thing: I don't have all the answers. Only God does—He's omniscient, remember? What I can share with you is what I have learned through Lutheran grade school, high school, college, and graduate school. And what I have learned through the toughest school of all—the school of hard knocks, more formally known as the school of experience. I've taught religion to teenagers in Lutheran high schools for many years. Based especially on those experiences, I want to explore with you the spiritual side of today's teenagers. God's best to you as you minister to youth!

A Spiritual Side

Like all of us, teenagers have four basic sides: the physical, emotional, mental, and spiritual. We can see a teenager's physical side, or body, when we meet. It is the "container" for their emotional, mental, and spiritual sides. We can get to know a teen's emotional and mental sides when we spend time together and talk. But we often have difficulty identifying a teen's spiritual side, or spirit. Jesus says in John 3:6, "Flesh gives birth to flesh, but the Spirit gives birth to spirit." It is sometimes tough for us to identify this spiritual side in teenagers since it is the part of themselves that they may be reluctant to talk about.

When working with teenagers, youth leaders often don't have to focus too much on the physical side; it's enough to provide the basic necessities of shelter, light, and a good nacho dip. We do, however, have to distinguish between their emotional and mental sides and their spiritual side. Naturally the question arises, *"Why do we need to make this distinction?"*

If we are going to minister to God's young people, we have to feed and nurture their spirits. We can't afford to make the mistake of offering only games, outings, and activities that touch a teenager's emotional and mental sides and believe that we have touched them spiritually. While there is nothing intrinsically wrong with a basketball game, a trip to an amusement park, or a camping trip, these events lack the ability to affect the spirit. We have to get young people into the Word in order to feed their spiritual side. Jesus says in John 6:63, "The Spirit gives life; the flesh counts for nothing. The words I have spoken to you are spirit and they are life." Why do we have to feed and nurture a teen's spiritual side? Because teenagers are starving.

Teen Spiritual Starvation

Like all Christians, Christian teens are sinful human beings; Ephesians 2:1 applies to them: "As for you, you were dead in your transgressions and sins." When God the Holy Spirit brings us to faith in Baptism, He makes us spiritually alive through the death and resurrection of Christ. Jesus says in John 3:5, "I tell you the truth, no one can enter the kingdom of God unless he is born of water and the Spirit." Furthermore, Ephesians 2:4–5 says, "But because of His great love for us, God, who is rich in mercy, made us alive with Christ even when we were dead in transgressions—it is by grace you have been saved." Thanks be to God that He sent His Son to live perfectly on our behalf, to die on the cross as the atoning sacrifice for our sins, and to rise again to bring us new life!

But like all Christians, Christian teens need to grow up in their faith! 1 Peter 2:2–3 says, "Like newborn babies, crave pure spiritual milk, so that by it you may grow up in your salvation, now that you have tasted that the Lord is good." God nurtures our spiritual life through the power of the Holy Spirit as we hear His Word and participate in the Sacraments. Just as a child is born and needs to be continually fed physically, so we all need to be reborn and continually fed spiritually! But many teenagers are starving spiritually; they are slowly dying because they are not nourished by ingesting the Word of God.

A 1999 poll from the Barna Research Group is revealing. According to this study, the following percentages of teenagers engage in weekly Christian activities:

Pray—89%

Attend church—56%

Attend Sunday school—35%

Read the Bible—35%

Attend youth groups—32%

Attend small groups—29%

If only about half (56%) of all teenagers attend church weekly, how are the other half getting fed spiritually? If only approximately a third of them show up for Sunday school or youth group, if only about a third read God's Word for themselves, what is happening to the spiritual growth of the other two-thirds of teenagers? If only one-third to one-half of your teens ate physical food weekly, you would be concerned. How much more concerned should we be that so many of our teenagers lack spiritual sustenance!

Spiritual Sustenance

Sustenance is, by definition, the sustaining or supporting of life or health. By this definition, many of our teens lack spiritual sustenance. They do not take in the "recommended daily allowance" of God's Word. I believe one main reason why teens (as well as adults) do not study the Bible is that they question both its truth and its relevance. Young people ask themselves these questions, even if they hide their questions from parents, pastors, and other adults:

    ✱ *Why is Scripture worth studying?*

    ✱ *Does it matter for life today?*

If we truly want to sustain teens' spiritual side, we need to help them answer these questions. But how do we do that?

Every school year I begin by discussing God, creation versus evolution, the inspiration of Scripture, cults, and other religions. I hope with this background to lay a sure foundation, one that will support a teen's faith. Rather than just teaching Bible stories right away, I try first to show my students that the Bible is both true and relevant. Many Christian teens in our world, as well as many adults, have these questions:

    ✱ *Is there meaning to life? (How did we get here? Why are we here?*
      What happens after death?)

    ✱ *Is there a God?*

    ✱ *Is there one true religion?*

    ✱ *Is the Bible reliable?*

With God's help we can provide spiritual sustenance, while supporting a teenager's spiritual life, by answering these basic questions. Why study Jesus' life if people doubt that there was a Jesus of Nazareth? Why read about God's plan for sexuality when people doubt the veracity of the Bible text? After addressing these issues, teenagers can study many different books or topics in the Bible, knowing that what they hold is God's truth.

In his classic book, *The Case for Christ*, former atheist Lee Strobel takes the reader through his personal investigation into the truth of the Scriptures and the reality of

Christ. Recently a new edition of this classic has been released. *The Case for Christ—Student Edition: A Journalist's Personal Investigation of the Evidence for Jesus* (Zondervan Publishing House: 2001) is designed to challenge postmodern teens in their thinking about God so they will examine the evidence for Christ themselves. While the book does contain some statements that may reflect a "decision theology" bias, it can be a useful tool for group study with teens.

The study *Solid Truth* (Concordia Publishing House: 1998) uses the Apostles' Creed as the basis for twelve sessions that examine the creed and its relevance to twenty-first century teenagers. Another great study for use with teens who are questioning the "correctness" of a religion is "Real Religion and Virtual Religion" from *Deceived by Darkness* (Concordia Publishing House: 2001).

Leading Youth Bible Study

BY TOM COUSER

So You're Going to Teach a Bible Class

Okay, so you have been recruited to teach the youth Bible class. Now that you've overcome the initial shock, the reality hits. The church has entrusted you with providing an ongoing ministry of nurture to the young people of the congregation. Overwhelming? Possibly. Impossible? Hardly! With the help of the Holy Spirit and through diligent study and planning, you can become a significant helping agent, an influencer in the lives of your students.

Bible study is an important element in the church's ministry to youth. Whether it's on Sunday morning, in an organized youth activity, or in a special setting, the circumstances are not as important as the fact that teenagers are studying the Scriptures. Bible study not only provides a learning opportunity, but equips young people for discipleship.

The teen years are unlike any other time in a person's life. Youth live in a fast-paced, constantly changing, high-energy world. For Christian young people, that means moving beyond the "childlike faith" taught in Sunday school. Young people are also progressing from having their parents as the primary influence in their lives to being pressured by peers to conform. Add to that the contemporary issues of society and the tensions of moving toward adulthood. For all these reasons, the teen years are a time of tumultuous change, a time when individuals need the security of a

Christian community more than at any time in their lives. Perhaps more than any other group, young people long for, even cry for, the assurance of the love of God that is revealed to them in the Bible.

Teachers as Facilitators

If Bible study is at the heart of the church's youth ministry program, then the people who lead Bible study are at the heart of a successful Bible study ministry. More than with any other age group, those who work with young people need special talents and abilities. They must be people who . . .

- *Care.*
- *Openly share their faith.*
- *Thirst to study the Scriptures themselves.*
- *Invest themselves in the lives of others.*
- *Listen.*

Perhaps we can think of the people who lead youth Bible study as facilitators rather than teachers. Teachers tend to tell; facilitators foster learning. With skilled use of techniques designed to involve the young people and with gentle direction, facilitators help their students discover on their own how the message of the Scriptures relates to their daily lives.

The Youth Bible Study Program

Youth Bible study very often occurs in a classroom during the Sunday school hour. But youth Bible study can happen in a number of settings and as part of a variety of activities. A complete youth ministry program also includes time for study of the Word during retreats, youth nights, social activities, and other events.

Whether your youth Bible study is a "once in a while" happening, an ongoing class, or both, you will want to give attention to all these events: getting into the study, the style of Bible study best for your group, selecting materials, the use of media, evaluation, and the like.

What Style of Bible Study Is Best?

The way you approach the sessions ought to fit the young people with whom you are working. The best style is the style that works with your class. If you are not sure what style will fit, you might try one for a couple of weeks, then move on to another. Variety will not only help you find out what works; it will add life to your study. (For additional help in finding various approaches, see the resources section.)

Large Group or Small Group?

Whether your group is large or small, size has its advantages. Large groups appeal to many young people; these groups create energy and foster a sense of belonging. But there may be problems. Large numbers limit opportunities for individual participation. In a large group, shy or reluctant learners may fade so quickly into disinterest that not even the skilled leader will be able to reach them. And when disinterest leads to absence, the large number of participants may make it difficult to even notice those who are no longer coming.

Small groups also have advantages and disadvantages. Watch teens. You will quickly notice that they tend to form small groups. Left on their own, they will cluster into groups of three or four and talk animatedly about whatever is on their minds. For that reason, many Bible studies suggest that larger groups break into smaller clusters so all can take part in the discussion.

It should be noted here that sometimes smaller congregations see themselves as disadvantaged when it comes to ministry to youth. Yet, unlike the large group that must be "broken down," the small youth group is already at its optimum size. It is basically the same individuals each week, which allows continuity of relationships and discussions. Also, there will not be the splitting up of friends that so often happens in large group "breakdown." There is less disruption and wasted minutes, so more energy and time can be spent on building relations and study. Still, some teens find themselves bored in relating to the same three or five or eight classmates with whom they've attended Sunday school all their lives. If so, consider having your small group join with other congregations for Bible study and social activities or mix occasionally in intergenerational events in your own congregation.

Finally, consider this additional benefit to the small group approach: small groups are more conducive to growth. It is much easier for youth to invite friends when there are fewer people to meet.

Lecture

Three basic approaches are useful with larger groups, but they all have drawbacks. One is to have a dynamic lecture. This usually requires a unique person with a very effective delivery. The lecture approach does not tend to involve youth in creative ways. Sometimes it will work—but rarely. If you decide to try it, know your material thoroughly and be prepared to include "audience participation" at strategic points. Ask a question. Have the group repeat an important phrase. Call for a show of hands. Remember, every lecturer wants to communicate, and communication is never a one-way street!

Relational Study

Another approach is called "relational" Bible study. This approach provides an opportunity to help participants grow in their faith as they relate to one another in groups of four to eight. The leader is responsible not to "teach," but to keep the groups moving along through the learning activities. Ordinarily, each member of the group receives a handout that gives the directions and asks questions. Participants are usually asked to record their responses to these questions before discussion begins. In this way, even if all do not speak, they have at least thought through the issues under study.

Relational Bible studies also have their limitations. Participants must be willing to work in a small group setting. Relational studies won't usually deepen a learner's cognitive knowledge of doctrine or Bible facts. And a very large group, broken into many clusters, can test even the ablest leader.

Active Learning

The active learning approach has grown more popular in recent years. Active learning blends the energy and enthusiasm of youth with their thirst for God's Word. The format ideally includes a group activity (game, role-play, etc.), an in-depth search of the Scriptures, and then a life application. Most active learning courses are short-term (four to six sessions). The teacher's guide usually contains reproducible student sheets, sometimes lowering the overall cost.

Again, this approach has its disadvantages. The leader must have a good deal of knowledge, both in biblical/doctrinal topics and in techniques for drawing the "debriefing" discussion to relevant conclusions. Without a skilled leader, students are likely to remember only the activity itself. On the other hand, a carefully constructed experience and discussion can touch students deeply, both in mind and heart.

Adding the Right Setting

A successful youth study group does not require a finely appointed classroom. But neither will it do to try to get things going behind the boiler in the basement or in the middle of a busy gymnasium. You will want the place in which your group meets to be roomy, reasonably private, comfortable, and well-ventilated. It might have tables, but small group discussions often happen best on the floor or in circles of folding chairs. Meeting in the same place every time lends continuity, but it is not necessary to claim a permanent "youth room" in the parish. Young people may wish to decorate the study group area with posters and other in-class creations. These may have to be moved periodically if the room must also serve other groups.

At Home

A room in the church is certainly not the only place where a youth study group can happen. A centrally located home with a large, comfortable room might create just the right atmosphere for your study group really to get going. Newcomers are likely to feel less strange, and a generous host might even provide refreshments. If you promise to clean up afterward, you might ask your host to let one of your group members bring a snack. Of course, a different home every week is a possibility too—but you will need effective communication to prevent total confusion on study group night.

School

Some high schools allow students to use classrooms for student-led Bible study before or after school. The setting might offer real advantages. Certainly the troubles and problems of the day will be fresh on the young people's minds. And at school it might be easier for participants to get the word out and invite their friends.

Alternative Settings

Finally, youth Bible study can happen anywhere there is room for a study group to gather. You might get a room in a local restaurant or get together at a community center. You might even provide materials and encourage your students to do their own study around the lunch table at school.

Consider Your Community When You Plan

As you set the time and location for your youth Bible study group, you will want to consider community factors that may influence your decision. What about the style of living in your community? Do families tend to be out of town at certain times? What implications does the lifestyle of your community have for your plans? Are there seasons of the year that demand more of your students' time? Are there traditions in your congregation that tend to affect your decisions? You will want to make the study group as convenient and accessible as possible.

Selecting Materials

Determining Needs

No matter how carefully you plan your session, the young people will quickly abandon the effort if it does not meet their needs. As you plan the content, you want to do more than select a topic that sounds interesting to you. You will want to make sure it also touches the interests and needs of your students. To make sure you are on the right track, you may want to include several of the young people early in the planning. They will not only let you know when your selection topics are right; they will also give valuable input on the format and style of the group.

There are several ways to gain insight into your students' areas of interest. First, you will want to know the young people on a one-to-one basis. And you will want to form those close relationships carefully. Some young people may be reluctant to share their feelings and their friendship with you. You will want to open avenues of communication by showing them that you are interested in them and their world. You might attend their high school sports events or speak to them personally before and after the study group. You might invite one or two to your home for lunch or for an evening. Ask them about the concerns of their friends and classmates. Listen. Give them a chance to be open with you. Progress on relationships might be slow, especially at first, but the closeness and trust that will result will make it possible for you both to plan and to lead your Bible study group more effectively.

In addition, you will want to be attentive to the other ways the concerns of the young people in your community are revealed. Read the local newspaper and your teens' school paper. Page through their yearbook. Check the library and magazine stand to find out what young people are reading. Watch their favorite television programs with them. And listen. What are they talking about? What's on their minds? Those are the things that might form the core of a helpful Bible study.

A more formal way to assess interest is to use a "needs assessment survey." This device will help you not only discover which concerns are most salient to your teens, but also gain some insight as to the intensity of the interest in various topics. (See the resource list at the end of this chapter.) Or you might devise a simple survey of your own. List topics that seem to be of interest. Let participants mark each on a continuum from "not interested" to "very concerned." A quick tabulation of the results will give you a profile of the interests of your young people. Resource Page 3 at the end of this chapter offers a sample needs assessment.

Finding Study Materials

Ideally, the areas of interest you discover ought to convert to Bible study-group topics. But unless you have time and skills to write materials of your own, you will have to find resources that will help you do the study with your young people.

The searching ought to be easy since Bible study resources for youth abound. A trip to your local Christian bookstore will offer many—perhaps many more than you can ever use. But you will want to do more than look for an interesting topic or pick some materials with catchy graphics. Not all materials are created equal. Some may be shallow. Many may badly confuse Law and Gospel or ignore the Sacraments. Others may lack Bible input altogether. Make your choices carefully. Look for materials that are Christ-centered and Bible-based in addition to being life-directed. If you are not sure what to select, ask your pastor or other parish professional for help.

In addition, you might check a publisher's catalog or Web site for a list of resources. Again, you will have to do some careful investigation. You cannot always take what the publisher says about the course as objective truth. You will want to look over a sample of the materials before ordering for the group.

In general, you can use every opportunity to become more familiar with current, helpful materials. Youth ministry workshops will likely review materials. And you might gain valuable insight into helpful resources from meetings with other youth leaders.

What to Look For

Be sure to enlist young people in your review of materials. They will be able to help you discover resources that are attractive, up-to date, and relevant to their lives.

Be especially aware of the leaders materials. In addition to the doctrinal criteria mentioned above, the study group session should be well laid out and carefully explained. You may want to ask some of the following of the materials:

* *Does the leaders guide proceed step-by-step through each session?*

* *Are there suggestions for optional activities that make the materials adaptable to your particular situations?*

* *Does the leaders guide list all of the materials that will be needed?*

* *Are the education objectives stated clearly and are they in line with the needs of the group?*

Most important, you will want to be sure that the material is a *Bible study* and not just a study that lists an occasional Bible passage. Is there a central emphasis on the Good News of salvation in Jesus Christ? Does God's Word form the center of each lesson? Does the study of the Word focus on God's gracious action toward His people? Unfortunately, many materials are very good at telling young people how they ought to behave but fail to remind them that God forgives them when they fail.

Finally, the materials should encourage our joyous response to God because of Jesus Christ. Worship suggestions will help young people express their gratitude to God and move them to carry their focus on the love of God in Christ into their lives.

Creating the Right Atmosphere

The spirit of the study group is important. The attitude of openness and trust that makes sharing successful is difficult to create and easy to destroy. Especially when you begin a new study group, you may be tempted to dominate the discussion. The silence of the students and their reluctance to participate may be just too much and you will feel forced to "fill in the blanks" with teacher-talk and arbitrary discussion. In doing so, you may be able to keep things going, at least for a time. But you will have taken responsibility for what happens during your time together. As a result, that fragile study-group spirit may be the victim of your good intentions. The openness and trust you hoped to foster may be lost. It is difficult to create a positive study-group atmosphere, but some of the following will help:

* *Don't try to make it your study group. Share the leadership, the decisions, the choices, the interaction.*

* *Remember that you teach individuals, not a group. Each participant comes to the study group with his or her own experiences, thoughts, needs, and feelings. You will want to do all you can to recognize the special gifts and abilities of each person and to make room for that person to participate in a way that is important.*

* *Try to spend some time with your students before and after the session. Time to talk to individuals is more important than setting out pencils or putting away the TV and VCR. Besides welcoming them, you can listen to what is going on in their lives. You may not be able to talk to each person each week, but all will feel they belong.*

* Consider building in some time for recreation (a volleyball game?) or time to socialize (a trip to the pizza place?) before or after your meeting. Or you might take turns providing a light snack during or after your study. Eating or playing together builds community more quickly than may be possible in a classroom setting.

* Provide additional resources for the participants. Have available youth ministry magazines, cassettes or CDs by contemporary Christian recording artists, and videos and books that relate to their life experiences.

* Build anticipation by giving suggestions for follow-up activities to be done during the week or offering a thought-starter for the subject of the next session.

In general, to create a positive study-group atmosphere let the students know that each is important to you and to the group, that their needs and concerns will be heard, that they have input into the way the study group will happen, and that they can feel comfortable about sharing with one another on a personal level.

The Story Session

Ready to Begin

* Start on time!

* Sit in a circle—on the floor if you can't move the chairs. Each person should be able to see all the others in the group. It is hard to talk to the back of someone's head.

* Begin with a welcome and a short devotional thought or prayer led by you or one of the young people. Ask volunteers to do the same for future study groups.

* Save announcements, plans for activities, business, and the like until the end. First things first.

Into the Study

Your group procedure may vary from week to week depending on the number of students and the subject you are studying. But keep the following in mind to facilitate sharing and discussion:

* Get to the center—the focus on Jesus Christ and His eternal love and forgiveness needs to come through, whatever the material or style of study.

* One rule: No one dominates—not even you. Everyone should be heard.

* Be enthusiastic. A joyful spirit is contagious. It may be easier to say than do—especially on those days when nothing has gone right. But it is important that you are excited and interested in the study. Your students will reflect your attitude.

* Keep things moving. Share the agenda with the students before beginning. Allow them to provide feedback and make adjustments where appropriate. However, if a participant has a pressing concern, deal with it before

beginning. If you don't allow them to deal with the issue, it will be on their mind while you try to lead the lesson.

* Make sure your study touches hearts and lives. At the end of the session, each student should know how the subject for the day relates to his or her daily living.

* Call people by name. Gently invite the participation of the shy or reluctant. Listen. Look each speaker in the eye. Ask questions until you are sure you understand what each person is saying.

* Put-downs don't belong in a youth Bible class. Teenagers live in a put-down culture. Provide words of encouragement and affirmation. Influence the participants to treat one another with respect. Even the most off-the-wall question deserves an answer. Even the most ridiculous idea needs to be heard. Foster an atmosphere of acceptance.

* Repeat key phrases to let students know when something important is being shared. For example, when you want them to hear a new point of view, you might ask, "How would you react to . . . ?"

* Fit the length of your study session to your topic and what you hope to accomplish. Don't try to fit your study into a certain length of time. There is nothing sacred about an hour. Stop when you are finished. Your students will let you know when you have reached the end. Use the rest of the time for informal talk.

* Use media to add variety. Carefully choose the videos, tapes, or CDs you will use. Make sure they fit the plan of the study group. Preview everything and make your own notes on what you see or hear. Use film listings and local media resource people (i.e., professionals in your congregation, public library staff) to help you use media effectively.

Evaluating the Session

Evaluate each meeting so you learn by experience as you plan future sessions. You will run across many evaluation devices, but these simple questions, directed to yourself or your students, might help you think through each session:

What did we learn (relearn) from the lesson?

How did our faith in Jesus or our faith in life grow?

What parts of the lesson went well?

How could we improve?

At first you might ask students to write responses each week. But when students know that their input makes a difference in study-group planning, they may be willing to give their evaluations openly and more informally.

In Conclusion

Like many of life's valuable experiences, leading the youth Bible study group will have its ups and downs. You will very likely go from feeling like super-teacher on one day to the pits of total failure on another. But, fortunately, our feelings determine neither the value nor the success of what we are doing. We have the assurance that as we help young people come into contact with the Word, the Spirit will be active there. The Lord's purposes will be accomplished through our sometimes effective, but never perfect, efforts. Miraculously, God forgives us too.

Where to Go for Help

District and Congregational Services—Youth Ministry Office
1333 South Kirkwood Road
St. Louis, Missouri 63122-7295
www.lcms.org

Concordia Publishing House
3558 South Jefferson Avenue
St. Louis, Missouri 63118
www.cph.org

Resources

Rydberg, Denny. *Building Community in Youth Groups* (Group Publishing: 1985).

Schultz, Thom, and Joani Schultz. *Why Nobody Learns Much of Anything at Church: And How to Fix It* (Group Publishing: 1993).

Yaconelli, Mike, and Scott Koenigsaecher. *Get 'em Talking: 104 Great Discussion Starters for Youth Groups* (Zondervan Publishing House/Youth Specialties: 1989).

The Youth Worker's Encyclopedia of Bible Teaching Ideas (Group Publishing: 1994).

Bible Study Group Needs Assessment

Rank each from 1–5 with 1 being your least preferred and 5 being your most preferred.

Group – What kind of a group would you like to meet in?

_____ *Small group of 5 to 8 people*

_____ *One large group*

_____ *Large group with small group break-out times*

_____ *Group with all guys/girls*

Location – Where would you most like to meet for Bible study?

_____ *Church*

_____ *School*

_____ *Someone's home*

_____ *Other location (specify) _____*

Time – When is the best time to meet?

_____ *Sunday morning*

_____ *Sunday evening*

_____ *Weekday morning, which day? _____*

_____ *Weekday evening, which day? _____*

Type of Study

_____ *Book of the Bible*

Which books would you most like to study?

_____

_____

_____

_____ *Topic*

What topics would you most like to study?

_____

_____

_____

_____ *Teachings of the Church*

Developing a Philosophy of Youth Ministry

BY CARL ELIASON AND AUDREY DUENSING-WERNER

First, let us ask the question, "What exactly is a philosophy?" A philosophy defines who you are and where you are going. A philosophy can be one-dimensional and closed in its focus; it can be intentional or unintentional; it can be driven by unrelated agendas; it can be exclusive in nature; or it can be integrated and multi-dimensional.

The second question to ask is, "Why is it important to define your philosophy of youth ministry?" Or, for that matter, "Why do we need to develop a philosophy of youth ministry in the first place?" The very answer to those questions could be, "If you do not know what you are shooting at, how will you know if you hit it?" In other words, if you do not have a central source to revisit whenever you develop or evaluate a ministry event, it will never be intentional.

A youth ministry philosophy defines your value system and priorities. From your philosophical framework, you set your vision, mission, and objectives. Youth leaders who focus their ministry and know their mission (what they are shooting at) have a foundation that is helpful in making decisions and setting goals.

Limited Philosophies

Everyone comes to youth ministry with his or her own philosophy. Your beliefs and experiences have shaped your philosophy, whether you know it or not! You bring that philosophy with you into any ministry setting. But unless your philosophy is both intentional and focused, it can lead to a ministry that is one-dimensional. One-dimensional youth ministries emphasize a particular aspect or goal and leave little room for growth for young people who may never fit into that box.

Examples of one-dimensional youth ministries include the following:

* *Ya'll Come Now, Ya Hear (program only)*

* *We Are the World (issue driven with mission trips and servant events)*

* *The More the Merrier (big events, gatherings, and huge crowds)*

* *Money! Money! Money! (fund-raisers)*

* *Tea for Two and Two for Tea (one on one)*

* *Country Club — the Youth Version (only those who fit in)*

* *Harry/Harriet Charisma (charismatic-leader led)*

* *Gilligan's Island (working only with* our *youth at* our *church with* our *events)*

* *The Bible Will Do It (focus on study without action)*

Ya'll Come Now, Ya Hear—A youth ministry philosophy based on the concept "If you build it, they will come." Most activities are offered at a specific site, perhaps the church building, on a set date and time, and only those who can make it then will ever get the opportunity to take part.

We Are the World—A youth ministry philosophy designed around mission trips, servant events, service projects, and disaster relief efforts. The ministry is set up primarily for these situations and nothing else. This ministry is powerful, as it develops strong bonds among youth who attend. It also helps to develop servant hearts for those who are ready to commit. However, some youth who are not quite ready for the deep commitment required are left out of the ministry completely.

The More the Merrier—A youth ministry philosophy in which participants come together only for big events like national youth gatherings, Youth Quakes, or huge group happenings. These events can get youth excited about worship and community, but many teens need a more intimate setting. The thought of huge events, where hundreds and thousands of kids gather in one crowded auditorium, scares them. Large events on the local level can create a great opportunity for inviting the unchurched, but unless leaders plan a way to incorporate visitors into the ongoing ministry, youth tend to cycle between the emotional highs of the big event and the emotional lows of everyday existence.

Money! Money! Money!—Yes, it's true; many youth ministries focus entirely on raising money for some trip or event. Sometimes the event or trip never works out. This style of ministry does provide some fellowship opportunities, but seldom do the young people grow in faith because they never gather around God's Word! Congregation members may even begin to see the youth ministry as a negative, always asking for money.

Tea for Two and Two for Tea—This philosophy is based entirely on one-on-one relationships between the youth minister and individual young people. In a wonderful way, one-on-one conversations do help youth leaders get to know the personality of each young person. This knowledge facilitates ministry. Unfortunately, the one-on-one approach also opens the door to burnout in the youth minister. It does nothing to get the young person connected, in a healthy way, to a community of believers. Consider the fact that while Jesus spent extra time with Peter, James, and John, He led a group of twelve as He modeled community and fellowship.

Country Club—Many youth ministry programs develop tight bonds between certain youths and then exclude others because the outsiders don't "fit in." Unfortunately, this can easily happen in congregations that support a Christian day school. The public school youth often feel like they are on the outside looking in, while the day school youth are so closely connected they do not notice the absence of some of their peers.

Harry/Harriet Charisma—There once was a youth minister who came in and "wowed the socks off" the youth. His/her personality drew them into events, and Harry/Harriet intentionally planned such events, knowing that the youth would come because they loved him/her. But what happens when "Harry/Harriet" leaves? Often the entire program falters because it was founded on a personality and not on Jesus Christ.

Gilligan's Island—This philosophy assumes the youth are "an island unto themselves." The ministry happens exclusively at *one* church, with *one* group of youth, without *any* outside resources, help, or interaction. No one else in the world realizes that people live on the island because the batteries in the radio that links them to the outside world are dead. Such isolation teaches a narrow view of the communion of saints and encourages a narcissistic self-focus.

The Bible Will Do It—This philosophy focuses primarily on the study of Scripture. Great! So many youth ministries fail to encourage teens to open the Bible and spend time pondering God's Word. However, if the youth spend all their time in study and never leave the safety of the Bible class, their faith is never tested, challenged, or applied. It remains largely academic, and its relevance is easily disconnected.

Effective youth ministry incorporates a variety of approaches, because a multidimensional program will attract and hold more youth and will foster greater growth in the individuals who participate.

An Integrated, Multidimensional Youth Ministry Philosophy

Having taken a look at what a youth ministry philosophy is and what it should *not* be, we can address the question "What is youth ministry?" Ministry occurs when God's people care for one another and share God's grace with one another in the name of Jesus Christ. Youth and adults, gathered together around God's Word, grow together in their faith. By the power of that Word, the Holy Spirit works through His faithful people as they share forgiveness, grace, compassion, celebration, and hope in Christ Jesus. Ministry occurs when God's Holy Spirit is present among His people in worship, study, and care for one another.

Youth ministry is ministry with and for youths. Since it is youth *ministry*—not youth football or youth dance class—theology must direct the philosophy that you develop. Use the Scripture passages below to help you shape a theological philosophy for your congregation.

Deuteronomy 4:9–14	*Ephesians 6:10–20*
Deuteronomy 6:5–7	*1 Corinthians 3:10–11*
Matthew 18:1–5	*Mark 9:42*
1 Peter 3:13–17	*Romans 12:2*
1 Timothy 4:12	*Psalm 71:17–18*
Matthew 28:18–20	*2 Timothy 3:14–17*
Psalm 78:1–8	*Titus 2:3–8, 15*
2 Timothy 4:1–5	*Ephesians 4:17–5:21*
Proverbs 22:6	

Baptism—identity formation as a child of God

One of the primary developmental tasks of adolescence is that of identity formation. Youth ministry should be about helping young people to identify themselves as children of God in Baptism. It should encourage frequent and meaningful participation in the Sacrament of the Altar, where the family of God gathers to receive forgiveness, strength, and hope. Youth ministry connects teens to the church in ways that nurture a sense of participation in the life of the congregation, a celebration of significant rites of passage, positive connection to traditions, and a growing understanding of their family and personal faith histories.

Servanthood—a grateful servant heart that imitates Christ

Developing opportunities for youth to serve the church, one another, and the larger community is essential. Society does well at encouraging acts of service during times of crisis, but youth ministry can nurture habitual servants, youth who help because service expresses the essence of who they are in Christ.

Character—practice Christian ethics and decision making in daily life

As all youth leaders know, young people ask tough questions about life issues and they look to the church for help in understanding the dilemmas the world throws at their feet. Young people need a safe place to explore values, doubts, and prejudices. Youth leaders can provide a thoughtful approach to life's paradoxes. Youth need help in exploring current events, and they need the guidance that Scripture provides in dealing with issues of right and wrong.

Disciple—have the tools and desire to spend time in God's Word

Youth ministry should be about training and equipping lifelong biblical scholars. Young people need to be exposed to the wide variety of study tools that are available to them as they search the Scriptures. Youth ministry can introduce youngsters to the wonder of a God who only grows more marvelous and wonderful as we come to know Him in Jesus Christ through His written Word and Sacraments.

Worship—an openness to, and an understanding of, different worship styles, traditions, and rituals, both new and old

Youth, just like adults, become creatures of habit. Both traditional worship forms, with their richness, and current musical styles, with their energy, offer merit and benefits. Youth leaders provide the understanding, education, and direction that will foster growth in worship.

Intergenerational—interaction to and with younger and older generations

Learning and teaching go hand in hand. Youth serve as excellent role models for younger children. Likewise, youth learn more about their own faith when they have opportunities to share that faith, learned in childhood, with others. They also grow through the rich nuggets of wisdom, the faith stories, and the commitment of more mature believers.

Fellowship—a Christian youth subculture

Peer groups. Fitting in. Relationships. As youth struggle with developing their own identity, relating to other people grows in importance. Teens need opportunities to interact within a safe, Christian setting. Youth ministry can provide this, both for members and visitors.

Evangelism—a focus on sharing the Gospel of Christ with family, friends, community, and the world

Many youth think of evangelism as banging on doors and beating their Bibles while standing on the street corner. Youth ministry should offer a more positive picture of outreach. Youth need opportunities to pray for the lost. They need encouragement in making godly choices and setting Christlike priorities. They need to learn the whys and hows of sharing the Christian hope with others in a caring, nonconfrontational way.

Stewardship—a willingness and desire to offer back to God the blessings they have received

In a secular society focused on self-indulgence and instant gratification, youth ministry can emphasize all aspects of self-management and self-control. The privilege of Christian stewardship may influence the type of fund-raisers the youth choose to do. Youth ministry can encourage young people to tithe some of their wages from part-time jobs. Youth ministry can also provide opportunities for young people to volunteer their gifts and talents in the church and community and to practice the care and management of God's creation. Finally, youth ministry can help young people appreciate the material gifts that God has given them.

Developing a Youth Ministry Philosophy of Your Own

Resource Page 4 asks important questions designed to help you develop your own youth ministry philosophy. That philosophy will not remain static. You will create and re-create it as you bring to it more experience and insight. The Lord will continue to guide this dynamic process, strengthening your ministry with young people. Ask Him to direct this process as you carry out your philosophy.

Resources

Benson, Peter L. *The Troubled Journey: A Portrait of 6th–12th Grade Youth* (Search Institute: 1993).

Benson, Peter L., Judy Galbraith, and Pamela Espeland. *What Kids Need to Succeed: Proven, Practical Ways to Raise Good Kids* (Free Spirit Publishing: 1998).

Benson, Peter L., and Eugene C. Roehlkepartain. *Beyond Leaf Raking: Learning to Serve/Serving to Learn* (Abingdon Press: 1993).

Benson, Peter L., and Dorothy L. Williams. *Determining Needs in Your Youth Ministry* (Group Publishing: 1987).

Borgman, Dean. *When Kumbaya Is Not Enough: A Practical Theology for Youth Ministry* (Hendrickson Publishers: 1997).

Carnegie Council on Adolescent Development. *A Matter of Time: Risk and Opportunity in the Nonschool Hours* (Carnegie Council on Adolescent Development: 1992).

Chromey, Rick. *Youth Ministry in Small Churches* (Group Publishing: 1990).

Clark, Chap. *The Youth Worker's Handbook to Family Ministry: Strategies and Practical Ideas for Reaching Your Students' Families* (Zondervan Publishing House: 1997).

Dettoni, John. *Introduction to Youth Ministry* (Zondervan Publishing House: 1993).

Dittmer, Terry. *Youth Ministry Sketchbook: 130 Practical Ideas for Ministry* (Concordia Publishing House: 1995).

Dryfoos, Joy G. *Adolescents at Risk: Prevalence and Prevention* (Oxford University Press: 1990).

Elkind, David. *All Grown Up and No Place to Go: Teenagers in Crisis* (Addison-Wesley: 1984).

Fields, Doug. *Purpose-driven Youth Ministry: 9 Essential Foundations for Healthy Growth* (Zondervan Publishing House: 1998).

Freudenburg, Ben. *The Family-friendly Church* (Vital Ministry: 1998).

Hardel, Richard A., and Merton P. Strommen. *Passing On the Faith: A Radical New Model for Youth and Family Ministry* (St. Mary's Press: 2000).

Hechinger, Fred M. *Fateful Choices: Healthy Youth for the 21st Century* (Hill and Wang: 1992).

Martinson, Roland D. *Effective Youth Ministry: A Congregational Approach* (Augsburg: 1989).

130 Ways to Involve Parents in Youth Ministry (Group Publishing: 1994).

Roehlkepartain, Eugene C., and Margaret Hinchey. *Youth Ministry That Makes a Difference: 30 Keys to Strengthening Your Congregation's Youth Ministry* (Search Institute: 1997).

Rydberg, Denny. *Youth Group Trust Builders* (Group Publishing: 1993).

Building Community in Youth Groups (Group Publishing: 1985).

Schultz, Thom, and Joani Schultz. *Involving Youth in Youth Ministry* (Group Publishing: 1987).

Strommen, Merton P. *Five Cries of Youth* (Harper and Row: 1988).

Varenhorst, Barbara B. *Training Teenagers for Peer Ministry* (Group Publishing: 1988).

Real Friends: Becoming the Friend You'd Like to Have (Harper and Row: 1983).

Vitek, John M., Keith M. McCormick, and Robert P. Stamschror. *A Companion Way: Mentoring Youth in Searching Faith* (St. Mary's Press: 1995).

Wyckoff, D. Campbell, and Don Richter, eds. *Religious Education Ministry with Youth* (Religious Education Press: 1982).

Zarra, Ernest J. *It Should Never Happen Here: A Guide for Minimizing the Risk of Child Abuse in Ministry* (Baker Books: 1997).

1. What key beliefs and experiences make up your philosophy of youth ministry? How does what you are doing now mirror your philosophy?

2. Evaluate what you are currently doing in light of your philosophy. What changes would you like to make in your philosophy or your approach? Why?

3. What do you hope your youth ministry will look like one day? Where would you like to be? (This is your vision.)

4. What do you need to do to get from where you are to where you would like to be? (This is your mission.)

5. Who needs to get involved in these efforts to develop and implement the philosophy?

6. What indicators will show your congregation's progress in implementing the philosophy? How and when will you measure progress?

The Role(s) of the Adult Youth Leader

BY PAUL SCHOEPP

Youth leaders come in all shapes and sizes. Sometimes the pastor takes primary responsibility for filling this role. At other times and in other congregations, the role of youth leader belongs to another professional worker—perhaps a teacher from the parish school or a director of Christian education. Sometimes the role of youth leader belongs to one or more adult volunteers in the congregation—perhaps the parents of a youth or another adult with a heart for young people. Finally, youth leadership can come from the youth themselves! (For more on that role, check out chapter 13, "Let 'em Lead.")

The primary focus of this chapter is on adult volunteers as youth leaders. It is not an exaggeration to say that adults—parents, extended family members, or other acquaintances—can play profound roles in the lives of young people and can make an impact that lasts a lifetime. I know that was true for me!

Let me start by thanking you for your involvement with youth in your congregation and the impact you have made and will make in their lives. If you are reading this chapter or attending a session to talk about these issues, you already *are* a leader in this area. You are a leader by virtue of your interest in and concern for young people. You are a gift from God and a precious asset in your congregation. Celebrate that reality and look forward to continued growth in the various roles you fill.

As I move along, I will first talk about what it means to be a leader—specifically what it means to be a servant leader. Then I will explore a cross section of the roles and responsibilities open to adults as they work with youth in their congregation. You will have an opportunity to explore which roles best fit your gifts and your ministry context. Periodically I will also ask you to pause to reflect and discuss. Discovering where you and the other adult leaders share the same perceptions and where you differ is an important part of growing together as a team and as a congregation. Let's get started.

(For a group session, the following questions are available on Resource Page 5A.) Describe the adults who were significant in your life as a teenager. What roles did they play in your life and in your faith development? Which adults have the primary leadership role for youth ministry in your congregation? Does your congregation's youth ministry belong primarily to professional workers of the congregation or to adult lay members? What does your response imply? What would the ideal scenario for adult leadership look like?

On Being a Servant Leader

Servant and *leader* are not words we often hear used together, yet when we do put them side by side, they describe wonderfully what it looks like to work with youth. We serve by leading and lead by serving because our Lord Jesus first loved and served us. In His cross, we receive forgiveness for our self-centeredness. His love moves us to compassion for others, particularly youth. We see opportunities to serve Jesus by serving youth—individuals for whom He also died. And we see opportunity to serve them by leading.

As servant leaders we imitate our Savior. Moved by His Spirit, our attitude mirrors Christ's attitude (Philippians 2:1–8). We serve not for the accolades we may receive, but with a sense of humility that recognizes youth and ministry as God's good and gracious gifts. Our leadership often involves putting the needs of the youth above our own. Thus, attitude is an important component of servant leadership.

Servant leadership also involves action. In Philippians we read that Jesus became obedient to death on a cross. In John 13:1–17 we read that Jesus washed His disciples' feet. He could not have chosen a more mundane or menial task. Washing feet was normally reserved for servants, and that is exactly why Jesus took on the task! He was demonstrating for His disciples and for us that leadership does not excuse us from doing the "dirty work." Sometimes we will set up chairs or mop floors. Tasks like these are not beneath us. They give us a chance to demonstrate love in action. Youth ministry provides many opportunities to act behind the scenes, to take on low-glamour servant roles.

Servant leadership involves our action in the mundane and the routine, but it also puts us up front at times. The gospels are filled with examples of Jesus teaching large crowds. He healed the sick and gave sight to the blind. He challenged the

Pharisees regarding their misinterpretation of God's Word. He also spoke very directly of His coming betrayal, death, and resurrection and set His face toward Jerusalem. His dynamic, public, and up-front leadership also served His Father in heaven and the world He was redeeming. Our willingness to lead Bible studies and set the direction for our congregation's youth ministry serves Christ every bit as much as our willingness to take the empty pizza boxes out to the trash. Youth ministry affords many opportunities to act in up-front servant-leadership roles.

(Also available on Resource Page 5A.) Read Philippians 2:1–8 and John 13:1–17 again. What other connections or insights can you make between servant leadership and the concepts of attitude and action? What other Bible passages inform your understanding of being a servant leader in youth ministry?

The Role of Articulating Purpose

Philippians 2:2 encourages God's people to be one in spirit and *purpose*. This is a critical role for adult youth leaders. Adults can help youth ministry function with perspective and balance. Too many youth groups want to focus almost exclusively on fellowship and fun, to the exclusion of the other vital elements that nurture vibrant and growing faith. Unfortunately, sometimes there is little to distinguish the church youth group from a social club at the local public high school.

The mission of the church, and consequently also of the church's youth, is much broader than mere fellowship. Take a look at Matthew 22:37–40; Matthew 28:19–20; and Acts 2:32, 42, 45–47. The passages from Matthew are Christ's words to His church in the Great Commandment and the Great Commission. The passage from Acts articulates how the early church put its faith into action. Christ's words and the actions of the early church can be distilled into five main areas:

> ✳ *Worship*
>
> ✳ *Service*
>
> ✳ *Evangelism or Witness*
>
> ✳ *Fellowship or Community*
>
> ✳ *Discipleship or Teaching*

A healthy youth ministry balances Christian living. Adult leaders can help youth see the broad picture of what youth ministry (and all ministry) should look like. Adults can help youths assess the current program and plan for more balance.

See Resource Page 5B. Write down words from each passage referenced above that match each of the five functions of the church. How does your congregation's youth ministry measure up? Do one or two functions exclude all the others? What might be done to correct that?

The Role of Risk Manager

Injuries to youths as individuals or to the congregation can come from many fronts. Sometimes the risk comes from people who work with youth—perhaps from youth counselors who are involved for the wrong reasons. Sometimes the risk comes from an outside group that has been contracted to provide a service for which it is not adequately prepared. At other times, the risk comes from the nature of the event or activity that is planned; a white-water rafting trip carries a higher risk factor than a Bible study and pizza feed in the youth room. Adult leaders have an important role to play in helping to minimize risk for both the youths and the congregation.

Parents entrust their children into our care, and we must take that trust very seriously. First, we take it seriously because each youth is a child of God, important to Him and to us. Second, we take risks seriously because a mishap caused by negligence could result in a lawsuit and financial ruin for a congregation. Risk management means anticipating what might go wrong and taking steps in advance to avoid those problems:

* *Consider background checks for all adults who work directly with youth.*
* *Check with the church insurance carrier to make sure you have adequate liability and vehicle coverage.*
* *Make certain that vehicles used for trips are mechanically sound.*
* *Make certain that drivers are 21 or older, have a clean driving record, and are fully insured.*
* *Require signed medical consent and liability waiver forms for all trips.*
* *Take along a first-aid kit.*
* *Take extra precautions for high-risk events such as rock-climbing or hayrides.*
* *Provide guidelines for appropriate behavior at events for both adult leaders and youth participants.*
* *Have an emergency plan in place and designate someone to implement it.*

What are the areas of risk in your congregation's youth ministry that need to be looked into and addressed?

The Role of Advocate

Have you ever felt ignored? that your plans and thoughts weren't considered worthwhile? It's not a good feeling, but young people sometimes experience it—even in church. Because of their age, because they are still growing in the ability to express themselves, because of their idealism, because of their impulsiveness, and because of the differences between contemporary youth culture and the world as adults see it, the ideas and actions of young people are sometimes discounted. Youth can be marginalized, taken for granted, and even ignored.

A youth advocate speaks on behalf of the youth and pleads their cause. Youth need such an advocate because the power and decision-making structures in most congregations belong to adults. Youth need adult advocates who will stand alongside them as they plan and implement their ministry, speaking for them in ways congregation leaders can understand. In these ways adult advocates serve as catalysts by helping youth identify and implement their ideas. Advocates locate resources to carry out ministry and help organize people and events. In addition, advocates pray on behalf of and with young people in the congregation.

(For a group session, see Resource Page 5C.) Describe a time (as a youth or adult) when you felt that you were not being taken seriously. How might an advocate have helped you in that situation? What biblical images of advocacy come to mind for you? (See Matthew 18:12–14; John 17:6–26; Romans 8:26–27, 34; or 1 John 2:1 to help you get started.) Where might advocacy make it possible for more effective youth ministry to occur in your congregation?

The Role of Mentor

Although an advocate cares about young people and ministry to youth, advocates usually deal with other adults in the congregation. In contrast, mentors in youth ministry relate and interact more directly with young people. The term *mentor* comes from Greek mythology. It refers to Mentor, the tutor to whom Odysseus entrusted his son Telemachus while Odysseus was absent. A mentor is thus a guide for the younger person or protégé. Unlike the situation in Greek mythology, parents need not be absent for a mentoring relationship to exist. Rather, the guiding role of mentors can supplement the primary parental role in important ways.

Some experts believe that the power of peer influence and of the media is greatly exaggerated. Research has shown that young people look first to their parents for guidance and advice. Next they look to other adults in their extended family—people like aunts and uncles or grandparents. Third on the list of influencers are significant adults outside the home—teachers, coaches, bosses, and adult leaders or mentors from the church youth group. Only when adults abdicate their important role in the lives of young people do peer and media influence shift to the forefront. Mentors play a vital role in helping young people make sense of their world.

The mentoring relationship is often very personal. Although there are many mentoring models, most of them involve a one-to-one relationship. One adult cannot mentor thirty youths. Instead, one adult usually works with two to six young people in an intentional and intensive way. Mentors and protégés typically grow very close, and lifelong relationships are often forged. In a mentoring relationship it becomes natural for a protégé to imitate his or her role model. The implications of this are quite sobering, since young people will not only imitate positive behaviors but will often pick up on the mentor's less desirable characteristics as well.

The Bible does not use the term *mentor*, but it does use the word *disciple*. We most often think of Jesus and the Twelve. Jesus called His disciples into a relationship that required their total commitment. He asked His disciples to leave home, family, and job to follow Him (Matthew 4:18–22). He asked His followers to deny themselves, take up their cross, and follow Him (Luke 9:23). Jesus spent time with the Twelve as He taught them many things in a small-group setting (Matthew 16:21 and Mark 4:34). Biblical pictures of how Jesus discipled (or mentored) His followers give us some insights as we consider serving as mentors. Jesus challenged His disciples, He spent time with them, and He explained things to them. But there is one difference we must clearly note: Jesus intended to transform His protégés into His own image; our role as mentors is to help our protégés become not more like *us*, but more like Christ (1 Corinthians 11:1; 2 Corinthians 3:18; and Ephesians 5:1).

(For group study, see Resource Page 5C.) Recall the significant adult with whom you identified earlier. Into which category would you place this person—parent, relative, or adult outside the home? Who were your adult mentors? What issues did you discuss with your mentor? How does interaction between Jesus and His disciples help you better understand the mentoring role?

The Role of Role Model

As an adult who works with youth, know that you will almost certainly become a role model. This is true whether you mentor three senior high kids or you coordinate transportation for sixty youth on the annual ski trip. Your leadership role puts you front and center in the eyes of young people as they begin to understand what it means to live out their Christian faith. Our "walk" and our "talk" need to be consistent so young people will see us "practicing what we preach." There are three important things for us to consider in this regard.

First is our corporate faith life. It is important for youth leaders to attend worship services on a regular basis. We need to hear God's Word preached and receive strength for daily living through participation in the sacrament of Holy Communion. In doing so, we also model for youth a healthy, growing faith life.

Second, group accountability for our personal growth in faith is important. Gathering together to study and discuss God's Word, asking questions, praying together, and holding one another accountable are all hallmarks of a growing Christian faith.

Finally, we need to develop personal spiritual habits or disciplines. This includes such things as personal Bible reading and memorization, meditation on God's Word, and time spent in personal prayer and reflection.

While we dare not flaunt these actions and activities before youth as an indication of our merit before God (Luke 18:9–14), we need to recognize that the Holy Spirit uses these opportunities to strengthen us for service. Scripture reminds us that we are like cities on a hill (Matthew 5:13–16). Our actions and lives can serve as salt and light for others in their faith walk.

Adults also need to model confession and forgiveness for young people. Each of

the role(s) of the adult youth leader

Basics

us will sometimes sin against the youth and adults we work with in what we say (or don't say), by a look we give, or by something we do (or don't do). One of the most powerful lessons I recall as a young person was my youth leader asking me for forgiveness after falsely accusing me of inappropriate behavior. That confession helped drive home for me the reality that we are all both sinners and saints. It also reminded me that the gift of God to His church is forgiveness through Christ. Only through the power of the cross are broken relationships restored.

(For a group lesson, use copies of Resource Page 5D.) Which of the three areas of your faith life (corporate, group, or individual) is strongest right now? Which is weakest? With God's help, how do you plan to address that? When is the last time you asked for or shared the gift of forgiveness with a young person in your congregation? What opportunities does God provide for you to share this gift?

The Role of Intentional Faith Talk

Kenda Creasy Dean and Ron Foster draw an interesting analogy in their book *The Godbearing Life.* They state that youth workers are to be like Mary. The Greek Orthodox church calls Mary *theokotos* because she literally bore God into the world. They suggest that our role, while not as literal as Mary's, is parallel. We, too, are to bear God into the world in our words and actions. We bear witness to God's mighty actions in our lives and in the world (Acts 1:8 and 1 Peter 2:9). But how do we do that?

In the days before the attacks on the World Trade Center and the Pentagon, I had invited a teacher and a pastor into one of the university courses I teach. I wanted them to share with the students what drew them into ministry, their training background, and the joys and frustrations of ministry. Their visit was scheduled for September 11, at about the time that the news of the attacks was just beginning to unfold. While we addressed the agenda for the day, we started off by talking about what their role as a pastor or teacher would be in light of this tragic news. The responses were startlingly similar.

In essence, both the pastor and the teacher said, "My role is to help people make connections between their faith and their life. I will read Scripture with my people (students), I will pray with them, and I will talk with them about what this means." During the days that followed, I reflected on those comments and came to realize that what these church workers said really summarizes our daily task as leaders in the church, whether we serve as pastors, teachers, DCEs, or volunteer adult youth leaders. It is our privilege and calling to help youth connect faith with the events of daily life, to bear witness to the reality of God in our lives.

I would like to suggest that our role does not change one bit, no matter what current events we encounter. Whether our youth are dealing with the news of another high school shooting or a terrorist attack; whether they have just won a track meet or landed their first job; whether they have "aced" a test or just broken up with a boyfriend or girlfriend—our role remains the same. We intentionally help young people interpret life in the light of faith and the hope that is ours in Jesus Christ.

(For a group session, use copies of Resource Page 5D.) What events are happening right now in your community and in the lives of your youth? How can you use these as opportunities for intentional faith talk? With whom do you talk about matters of faith and life?

Which Role(s) Is/Are for Me?

We've looked at a number of different roles adults can play in congregational youth ministry, but the list is far from exhaustive. As we conclude this session, take several minutes to reflect on the role(s) of adults in youth ministry.

(For groups, provide copies of Resource Page 5E.) What role(s) would you add to those we've already covered? Label and describe them. Can you think of any biblical examples for the role(s) you just identified? Choose the two or three roles that you believe are most important. What is it about them that makes them important? How will you invest yourself in carrying out one or more of these roles in your church's youth ministry?

You may have identified other roles, including teacher, counselor, transportation coordinator, planner, leadership developer, and friend. All these roles and more are valid. Perhaps as you consider all these roles and couple them with the many expectations expressed by youth, the church staff, and other congregation leaders, you may feel a bit overwhelmed. Don't panic! Pick the one or two roles that match your gifts and abilities and then get involved at a level you are able to sustain.

In his book, *Purpose-driven Youth Ministry,* Doug Fields suggests that the church often limits the ability or willingness of people to serve by taking an all-or-nothing approach—either you lead a weekly Bible study of senior high youth and take part in all of their fellowship and service events or we can't use you! An alternative approach recognizes various roles, each with a valid place in the total scope of ministry. Some in the congregation can serve as part of a cheerleading team that celebrates, lifts up, and advocates for youth ministry. Others in the congregation may choose to provide the financial support and resources necessary for youth ministry, even though they have little hands-on contact with the youth. Still others willingly provide prayer support. Finally, some adults will have the primary, face-to-face contact with youth. Some of these people will function well in large group settings and will take up-front roles with lots of youth. Other adults will prefer a more intimate, small group setting or will choose one-to-one ministry. Just about everyone can serve in youth ministry. The trick is finding each person's interests and abilities and defining a role that fits.

I hope this article has helped you discover or rediscover some of the roles available to you in youth ministry. I pray you have given serious consideration to one or more of them. Now I hope you and your congregation's leaders develop a job descrip-

the role(s) of the adult youth leader

Basics

tion based on what you have discovered.

At the very least, a job description should outline the parameters of responsibility and the time commitment required to carry out a particular role in youth ministry. Ideally, the job description will also address the necessary qualifications, talents, and spiritual gifts. The description should also talk about the youth leader's responsibility to the congregation through lines of accountability and the congregation's accountability to the youth leader through resource availability and equipping opportunities. A concise job description will serve as an excellent tool for recruiting adults into youth ministry roles. It will also serve well as a tool to help evaluate the overall effectiveness of the congregation's youth ministry.

(For groups, use Resource Page 5E.) Take some time to review youth ministry job descriptions for your congregation. Do they meet the criteria given above? How is a written job description more helpful than an oral one? If your congregation does not have job descriptions for youth ministry, take some time to develop one for each of the roles you have identified as important for your congregation.

Closing Thoughts

Serving in an adult leadership role in your congregation's youth ministry can be a demanding and sometimes frustrating task. Youth leaders feel the constraints of time. On occasion, they can feel unappreciated. Sometimes they experience the frustration of minimal congregational support. But youth ministry also offers an incredible set of rewards! In adolescence, young people make incredibly important decisions about their faith and life. What a privilege to serve and lead by taking part in that process. No joy compares with standing alongside young men and women as they grow in their faith and explore the gifts and abilities God has given to them!

If you are in a group, pray together now. Give everyone an opportunity to offer one or more of the following petitions or petitions of your own choosing:

  * *Thank God for the opportunity to serve as adult leaders among His people. (Share what you appreciate about youth.)*

  * *Confess times you have not carried out to the best of your ability the roles and responsibilities entrusted to you. (Share your own areas of struggle.)*

  * *Thank God for His forgiveness in Jesus Christ for times of sin and failure.*

  * *Ask that through His Holy Spirit, God would empower your ministry to and with youth. (Note both your areas of strength and the areas where you need to grow.)*

  * *Ask all these things in the name of Jesus Christ, our Lord and Savior—a servant leader who serves and leads us.*

Resources

AdvoKit: A Resource for Developing Advocates for Young People (LCMS Youth Ministry Office: 1985).

Crabtree, Jack. *Better Safe Than Sued* (Group Publishing: 1998).
A resource that covers the bases on risk management and liability.

Dean, Kenda Creasy, and Ron Foster. *The Godbearing Life: The Art of Soul Tending for Youth Ministry* (Upper Room Books: 1998).
Dean and Foster lift up the relational (incarnational) nature of ministry to youth and highlight the importance of the leader's faith walk.

Fields, Doug. *Purpose-driven Youth Ministry: 9 Essential Foundations for Healthy Growth* (Zondervan Publishing House: 1998).
The title of this book makes its focal point quite evident. An excellent resource for helping talk about the "why" of ministry.

Olson, Ginny, Diane Elliot, and Mike Work. *Youth Ministry Management Tools: Everything You Need to Successfully Manage and Administrate Your Youth Ministry* (Zondervan Publishing House/Youth Specialties: 2001).
A book targeted at the overall administration of youth ministry, with some helpful chapters on risk management.

Rice, Wayne. *Junior High Ministry: A Guide to Early Adolescence for Youth Workers* (Zondervan Publishing House/Youth Specialties: 1997).
A practical book that makes a case for early adolescent youth ministry, identifies developmental characteristics of junior high students, and discusses adult roles and mentoring.

Intensive Caring: Practical Ways to Mentor Youth (Group Publishing: 1998).

Describe the adults who played significant roles in your life as a teenager.

Describe their roles in your life and in your faith development.

Which adults have the primary leadership role for youth ministry in your congregation?

Does your congregation's youth ministry belong primarily to called workers of the congregation or to adult lay members?

What are the implications of your response, and what would the ideal scenario for adult leadership look like for you and your congregation?

Read Philippians 2:1–8 and John 13:1–17.

What other connections or insights can you make between servant leadership and the concepts of attitude and action?

What other Bible passages inform your understanding of being a servant leader in youth ministry?

Articulating Purpose

Match each of the five functions of the church to the words from the selected verses given below.

Matthew 22:37–40   Matthew 28:19–20   Acts 2:32, 42, 45–47

Worship

Service

Evangelism or Witness

Fellowship or Community

Discipleship or Teaching

How does your congregation's youth ministry measure up?

Do one or two functions exclude all the others?

What might be done to correct that?

Risk Manager

What are the areas of risk in your congregation's youth ministry that need to be looked into and addressed?

Advocate

Describe a time (as a youth or adult) when you felt that you were not being taken seriously. How might an advocate have helped you in that situation?

What biblical images of advocacy come to mind for you? (See Matthew 18:12–14; John 17:6–26; Romans 8:26–27, 34; or 1 John 2:1 to help you get started.)

Where might advocacy make it possible for more effective youth ministry to occur in your congregation?

Mentor

Recall the significant adult with whom you identified earlier. Into which category would you place this person—parent, relative, or adult outside the home?

Who were your adult mentors?

What issues did you discuss with your mentor?

How does the interaction between Jesus and His disciples help you better understand the mentoring role?

Role Model

Which of the three areas of your faith life (corporate, group, or individual) is strongest right now?

Which is weakest?

With God's help, how do you plan to address that?

When is the last time you asked for or shared the gift of forgiveness with a young person in your congregation?

What opportunities does God provide for you to share this gift?

Intentional Faith Talk

What events are happening right now in your community and in the lives of your youth?

How can you use these as opportunities for intentional faith talk?

With whom do you talk about matters of faith and life?

Which Role(s) Is/Are for Me?

What role(s) would you add to those we've already covered? Label and describe them.

Can you think of any biblical examples for the role(s) you just identified?

Choose the two or three roles that you believe are most important. What is it about them that makes them important?

How will you invest yourself in carrying out one or more of these roles in your church's youth ministry?

Take some time to review youth ministry job descriptions for your congregation. Do they meet the criteria given in the lesson?

How is a written job description more helpful than an oral one?

If your congregation does not have job descriptions for youth ministry, take some time to develop one for each of the roles that you have identified as important for your congregation.

Developing a Support System

BY SUE STEEGE

All Alone?

"That mailing should have gone out two weeks ago," said Mr. Jones. He was irritated. "My Joey has a packed schedule. Without better notice, he can't fit youth events into it!" As Debbie hung up the phone, her heart sank. It was the third phone call of the night from a frustrated parent. Pastor Schulz had asked to speak to her too. She knew *that* wasn't good news. Then there was the gossip about the mess the youth group left in the kitchen after the Easter Breakfast. Feeling very alone, Debbie wondered again whether youth ministry was the place for her. "Maybe I should just give it up," she thought.

A Support System Could Help

Debbie needs a support system! Whether you are a volunteer youth leader or a paid professional, a support system provides a soft place to fall and a good place to stand. A support system is a multifaceted set of connections, people who provide honest feedback, nurture, and prayer support for both the youth leader and the congregation's youth ministry. A healthy support system can help make youth ministry more effective. But support systems do not just happen. Learning to develop, nourish, and use a support system is a critical skill for those who minister to youth.

The fact that youth leaders need support should not come as a surprise. Our Christian faith consists of connections. God's connection to us is forged at the cross and personalized in our Baptism. This connection links us to all the other believers in the family of God. Many biblical images reinforce this concept of connection:

* *The church as the body of Christ (1 Corinthians 12; Romans 12)*

* *Believers as "living stones" built together into "a spiritual house" (1 Peter 2)*

* *The "one bread" and "one body" of the church, united at the altar as Christ nourishes us with His own body and blood (1 Corinthians 10:16–17)*

Simply put, there should be no "lone rangers" in youth ministry. That kind of approach models a faulty picture of ministry to the young people we serve. It keeps us from getting the support we need to function well in ministry—and in life! A healthy support system provides the following:

* *Helpful feedback. You need clear and honest feedback about your ministry style, the program's effectiveness, your leadership skills, and your relationships with young people and parents.*

* *Prayer backing. You need allies who will pray for your young people, those who minister with them, and the overall youth ministry of the congregation.*

* *Fellowship. You need space and time in your life for fun and relaxation.*

* *Opportunities to refocus. You need to ask how youth activities and leadership match your mission and vision for youth ministry.*

* *Advocacy. You need supporters who will speak up for both young people and youth ministry within the congregation and community.*

Developing this kind of support system is critical for both professional church workers and volunteers. The system may be formal (staff, youth board, church council, "personal board of directors," and so forth) or informal (friends, family, acquaintances). How do you develop and cultivate such a system? It begins with our attitudes, which in turn shape our behavior.

Attitudes

1. It's okay to ask for help.

Many times, people in ministry feel isolated and alone. They fear that asking for help will imply that somehow they don't "have it all together." In reality, no one has it all together. Even the most accomplished leaders know the value of continued learning, growth, and building on past success and failure. When we realize that it's okay to ask for help—that, in fact, those who are wise treasure the help of others—we have one essential attitude necessary for developing a healthy support system.

2. Feedback can be sought, not feared.

Feedback scares insecure folks. Sometimes youth leaders feel as though "everyone is out to get them." Ministry consultant Les Stroh taught me this: "Feedback is really 'A' telling 'B' about 'A.'" Often, someone's evaluation reveals more about the evaluator than about you! This means you can ask for feedback and receive it not as the absolute truth, but as part of a bigger picture. Feedback is information that can help you understand how you are received. It does not mean that the other person has it exactly right. Ask for a direct, clear response. For example: "Will you listen as I lead this game and tell me if you think my directions were clear and easy to understand?" This kind of specific question turns feedback into a wonderful gift, one that can help you grow as a person and as a youth leader.

3. Prayer makes a difference.

Our heavenly Father has promised to hear and answer the prayers of His faithful people. He truly does what He has promised! Ask others to pray for you, for the young people, and for specific youth events. Prayer is a wonderful gift! Make prayer a regular part of your own life—asking that God would help you be more aware of the constant support that He gives.

4. Parents are not the enemy.

Too often youth leaders see parents as adversaries in youth ministry. Take a hard look at parents and realize that they are, hands down, the frontline youth ministers in your congregation. They live and breathe "youth ministry"! Your task is to partner with them in ministry to their kids.

5. Many people want to be supportive.

When you feel all alone, remember the people who support you and your ministry. You may not know these individuals, but they exist. Seek God's guidance as you open your eyes and your ears to find these individuals.

6. Developing a support system is a process, not an event.

Developing a support system does not happen overnight. It is a long-term process that involves commitment of time and energy. Plan to take specific action to nurture your support system over weeks, months, and years.

Take Action!

1. Tell the stories!

You can't talk about youth ministry and your young people enough! Tell everyone you know how youth ministry is going in your congregation. Have youth share with the congregation their experiences at youth trips and servant events. Talk about youth ministry with the church staff, especially the senior pastor; with parents; with your friends; and with others in congregational leadership. Many times people are unaware of the great things that are happening with youth. When they begin to hear the stories, they can't help but support the ministry.

2. Set up feedback loops.

Build feedback loops into designated youth events. Ask young people for feedback about the event. Ask counselors how they think a specific event went. Identify goals before the event and ask for feedback related to those goals. For example, your goal is to create a welcoming place for youth who are not members of your congregation. After an event, you ask questions related to that goal, for example, "How did we welcome visitors to our event?" "What did we do that may have made visitors feel left out or on the outside?" As you use feedback loops, you will likely see greater support from people because they will perceive you as someone who wants to work toward excellence in youth ministry.

3. Have fun!

Make sure you reserve space and time for fun in your life. Set appointments with friends or family to do something purely for the fun of it. Taking time to be "off task" is an important stress reliever and strength-builder.

4. Consider enlisting a personal board of directors.

Develop a group of individuals willing to help you stay true to God's calling in your life. These individuals will help you explore who and what God wants you to be. Some of these people may be friends or relatives; some may be good at asking you the hard questions; some might have expertise in the areas of your life goals. Ask these people for feedback about where you are headed professionally, personally, and in ministry. Allow these individuals to help you think through the "big picture" questions of life. Ask them to hold you accountable. Ask them to pray with you and for you. Try to meet with your personal board of directors at least two to four times a year.

5. Listen to parents.

Find ways to communicate with parents. Start a regular e-mail letter to parents that invites their responses. Listen to how each family reacts to your plans. Ask parents how their kids are responding to youth activities. Ask how you can help them in their role as parents. Parents can be a great and integral part of a youth leader's support system.

6. Ask for support.

Recruit advocates from among your friends, staff, or board members. Ask that they support the youth ministry in their conversations, prayers, and finances. Develop opportunities to remind people about how youth ministry furthers the total mission of the congregation, and listen to the connections others make. Don't be afraid to ask for support. You will be much more likely to receive it if you ask for it!

Don't miss out.

A healthy support system is life-giving. God works to serve us through the support of fellow believers. Developing a support system is worth the effort. Don't miss the chance to grow in ministry by using this helpful tool.

Think It Through

* *How might you seek feedback, prayer, fellowship, opportunities to refocus, and advocacy for yourself and your ministry?*

* *Take time to study some of the Scripture passages that outline our connections with other believers and how foundational they are to life as a Christian. Start with 1 Corinthians 12; Romans 12; or 1 Peter 2.*

* *How might your development and nurture of a support system model mature Christianity for the youth with whom you serve?*

* *Think of five or six people you trust. Ask them to give you some clear, direct feedback.*

* *How might you improve your communication with youth, parents, supporters, and your congregation?*

Resources

Ken Blanchard, et al. *High Five!: The Magic of Working Together* (Morrow: 2001).

Bolman, Lee G., and Terrence E. Deal. *Leading with Soul: An Uncommon Journey of Spirit* (Jossey-Bass: 2001).

Simpson, Amy, ed. *No More Us and Them* (Group Publishing: 1999).

connections

7

Congregational Connections

BY DAVE RAHBERG

Introduction

How does youth ministry connect to a congregation that has people of all ages and a variety of needs? How do voters' assembly members justify expenses related to initiating and supporting youth ministry? How does the congregation or the community benefit if one person provides full-time leadership for youth ministry? How can youth ministry participants encourage spiritual growth in the congregation?

The connections between youth ministry and the congregation provide critical opportunities for building the kingdom of God. Youth ministry provides a learning environment for discipleship and service within the church. Youth ministry leaders use God's gifts to empower youth and adults for ministry within the community.

Youth Ministry's Connection to the Congregation

Youth ministry, like ministry for adults, focuses on relationships. When I reflect on these relationships, I recall some "ministry memories" from my years in the congregation. Some of these memories encourage, while others may motivate you to prayer and service.

❋ *Maggie's husband of 46 years had gone to heaven; her children live 700 miles away. She longed for the warmth of a hug and the sight of a loving smile. The youth invited themselves to Maggie's house to clean up the yard and make a few repairs. Maggie looked forward to their visit. She baked cookies and cleaned the house. Ever since that weekend, the youth greet Maggie on Sunday mornings at church. The youth discovered that, like themselves, Maggie needed a little encouragement.*

✳ *The freak accident occurred during fall semester. At drill-team practice, Kathy's flag descended too fast and delivered a debilitating blow to her temple. Upon examination, doctors discovered that Kathy's injuries threatened her intellect and personality. Members of Kathy's congregation prayed, spoke words of comfort to her family, and counted good health as a daily blessing. Kathy and her family shared the stories of her recovery and progress with well-wishers. Within two years of the accident, Kathy won a full scholarship to college.*

✳ *For one church family, something went terribly wrong. Contacts developed on the Internet separated Mandi from her parents. Mandi ran away from home to adopt a lifestyle that deprived her of years of joyful memories and opportunities. The members of Mandi's home congregation watched, cried, prayed, and encouraged her family while they waited for the "prodigal daughter" to return. Reconciliation finally came almost three years after the ordeal began.*

✳ *September 11, 2001—attacks on the nation's people and strategic buildings brought all of America together. Americans and others around the world expressed outrage at the attacks. Americans turned to God in prayer. The president asked us to pray. We knew a military response would follow once a plan was developed. The youth who ushered us into church one week could report for active military duty the next.*

Young people in your church can push you to move beyond your comfort zone to a new level of trust in God. The body of Christ gathers in joyful and difficult times, renewed through the Holy Spirit's power. Through God's Word and Sacraments, the Holy Spirit announces His presence in the hearts of believers of all ages. This same Holy Spirit invites those outside the body of Christ to enter into a renewed relationship with our Creator through faith in Jesus. To help you better understand the connection between youth ministry and the congregation, the remainder of this chapter will consider the following:

✳ *Effective youth ministry leads youth and adults into mature discipleship.*

✳ *God Himself works to establish these relationships with His people.*

✳ *Work to accomplish God's purposes through your congregation.*

✳ *God provides resources for youth ministry.*

✳ *Youth ministry benefits the whole community.*

As you explore these issues, consider your young people, their families, their friends, and the people they meet. God entrusts these young believers to your care. He wants to nurture their faith. The congregational connection to youth ministry becomes a matter of stewardship—God provides the people, the spiritual gifts, and the resources to accomplish His purpose; you work to utilize the resources He provides for the benefit of the kingdom of God.

Effective Youth Ministry Leads Youth *and* Adults into Mature Discipleship

How does your congregation intentionally help families nurture faith in their children and youth? Consider those families. Healthy youth ministry recognizes new ways to share with teenagers, their families, and their friends the life-changing message of God's grace.

Study the demographics of your youth. Consider the percentage of high school athletes, band members, honor-roll students, and working youth. Which youth affiliate themselves with gangs, drop-outs, or other troubled youth? Will your young people attend community college or a university, join the military, or start working after high school? What problems challenge youth in your community? What challenges exist for the parents of your young people? Are the parents in conflict with each other or with their teen? Once you gain an understanding of needs, plan to meet those needs. Activities designed for youth and adults provide opportunities to minister to both. Plan events that expose youth and adults to the healing Word of God.

Who in your congregation and community needs youthful energy and encouragement in their lives? What congregational connections could provide those needing extra love an encounter with young Christians who want to do something meaningful? Explore ways to bring youth and people with special needs into relationships that reflect God's loving care.

God Himself Works to Establish Relationships with His People

God's powerful Word changes His followers' attitudes and behaviors. Through His people, God directs the ministry He wants for His kingdom in your congregation. True ministry does not involve mere acts of dutiful obedience to our Redeemer. God does not need us to do ministry for Him. Rather, He invites us to join His ministry in response to His love for us.

God changes our hearts as He prepares us for eternal life with Him. "No one can come to Me unless the Father who sent Me draws him, and I will raise him up at the last day" (John 6:44). God works in the hearts of your members as they grow in faith, mature in their relationship with God, and respond to the needs of others in response to God's love for them. Ask God to open your eyes to recognize His work in your youth ministry. Only God can create within us a hunger for an intimate relationship with Himself. God motivates us to repentance and spiritual restoration through His Word. The Holy Spirit empowers believers of all ages to use His gifts to build up the body of Christ.

Work to Accomplish God's Purposes through Your Congregation

Leadership requires vision. This *vision* includes the ability to recognize God at work through His people, using their zeal for service, His gifts, and His resources. Allow your youth to serve where their individual gifts and talents can be effective. See God at work in His people. Identify needs beyond current ministries, and look for possible congregational connections. Talk about what you see God doing among His people of all ages. Give God glory for the work He does in and through His people. Endorse ministries that allow God's people to effectively use the gift of His Word to bring others into a saving relationship with Christ.

Leaders articulate ways that youth ministry supports the congregation's efforts to make a difference for the kingdom of God. Identify the resources available and needed to fulfill these ministries. Pray, encourage, and listen for God's direction concerning His people. Evaluate ministry effectiveness and potential for growth in the kingdom of God. Make the hard choices about when to start and end projects. Follow up and assist frontline volunteers with their efforts. Look for ways to say "Yes!" to God's direction for His people.

Don't overlook your personal faith walk as you provide direction to young people. The power of God's Word and Sacraments sets you free to be God's servant-leader in your congregation. As a leader, you bring the truth of the Gospel into the lives of the people that God puts in your care for His name's sake. Take time for your own spiritual development through regular study of God's Word and participation in the Sacraments.

God Provides Resources for Youth Ministry

Human Resources

At our Baptism, the Holy Spirit comes to dwell in our hearts. This same Spirit gives each of us unique gifts, given for the benefit of the body of Christ. The Old and New Testaments both bear witness to God working through His people throughout their lifetimes. Consider how God used Joseph, Samuel, David, Timothy, and Titus to build His kingdom. Even as young people, they served the Lord and others.

Youth ministry participants can have both long- and short-term opportunities for involvement, depending on their interests, time, and spiritual maturity. Short-term, high-impact projects are often filled with immediate opportunities for participants to meet others and try on different areas of service. Individuals with special skills will often give a short-term project priority in their lives. Some participants may be willing to make long-term commitments because of the needs addressed.

To facilitate spiritual growth, match mature Christian adults with young people in mentoring relationships. Through these relationships, the kingdom of God is strengthened and renewed and future church leaders are nurtured.

Basics

Recognition of God's power at work in His people includes celebration. Take pictures, publish stories, and provide opportunities to celebrate God's work through His people. Send thank-you notes to people who make themselves available to serve God. When adult members of the congregation see young people in ministry, they gain a sense of hope for the future of the church.

Financial Blessings

Effective youth ministry involves more than a series of fund-raisers for out-of-town celebrations or service projects. Two or three major fund-raisers each year provide funds more effectively than selling "widgets" during the monthly combination car wash and bake sale. Continuous fund-raising promotes the appearance that youth ministry focuses solely on money.

A powerful connecting point between congregations and youth ministry participants concerns the stewardship of funds generated by youth. Families with youth experience frequent stresses due to the financial drain of a teenager's extracurricular activities. Most parents look for ways to teach responsible stewardship to their growing children.

Fund-raisers provide opportunities to teach biblical stewardship principles. You might encourage youth to designate a "firstfruits" percentage (many groups choose 10 percent) from each fund-raiser for a congregational mission focus. Some groups credit the remaining money raised to individual accounts for each participant based on the number of participants or hours worked. Each young person can then use his or her account for congregational ministry events. For example, a youth could access his or her account to pay for a skating party, camp-out, youth gathering, retreat, choir tour, service project, or even to sponsor guests for youth activities.

When young people graduate from high school, any excess money in an individual's account can continue to support youth ministry. Transfer the leftover funds to that individual's next oldest sibling or to an assistance fund for others. Explain the youth fund to parents each year. A responsible youth and an adult could work together to manage the account.

Youth ministry also requires funding through the congregation's budget. This budget should include financial resources to establish and maintain a physical space for youth ministry, provide a resource library, purchase equipment that will support youth ministry endeavors, and purchase materials for spiritual development. In addition, the congregation's budget should provide funding for adult leader expenses, training, resources, and team development. Invite individuals who say, "Youth ministry leaders take church-funded vacations," to give up an afternoon, weekend, or vacation time to assist with the next lock-in, fund-raiser, service project, retreat, or trip.

The congregation's budget for youth ministry reflects the church's commitment to disciple children in the Christian faith as promised at their Baptism. The congregational budget for youth ministry teaches Christian stewardship principles to youth ministry participants. Because they are second only to retired adults in the amount of discretionary money available each month, teens possess a powerful financial voice. Encourage your youth to see the church budget as a means to return to God the financial blessings He has given them.

When people see God working, they respond in generous ways. Given the opportunity, some will volunteer to provide financial and/or professional help. Some individuals may want their contribution to remain anonymous, while others may help by lending their support in a public way. Ask donors how you may best acknowledge their gifts.

Beyond fund-raising and the church budget, significant "third source" funding opportunities exist. These include gifts from fraternal insurance agencies, private donors, and community agencies. Most fraternal benefit societies as well as major corporations make funds available for a variety of projects, including matching funds, challenge grants, member/employee contribution matching, percentage of sales, and one-time gift grants.

Physical Property

In some communities, nonprofit agencies receive gifts of equipment and supplies from companies going through changes in their organization or product lines. Items available can include office equipment, computers, blankets, or baby- and infant-care items. Use these items to equip your meeting space, mission teams, or other congregational ministries. Encourage church members who work for companies that make items available to nonprofits to let you know when materials become available.

Youth Ministry Benefits the Whole Community

Christ Jesus gave the Great Commission in Matthew 28:19–20. Christ's church makes disciples, baptizes them in the name of the triune God, and teaches them God's way for their lives. God's Word encourages us as we undertake these responsibilities. Your congregation will carry out Christ's commission in ways unique to your setting and circumstances.

Your congregation's organizational structure should invite participation by youths, encourage personal responsibility, and make good use of God's gifts. Your organization can free youth and adults to serve with joy and meaning. Equip the people involved in youth ministry with the skills, knowledge, and resources they need to be successful in that ministry.

Conclusion

Youth ministry and relationships in the kingdom of God today lead to mature discipleship for a lifetime. Effective youth ministry involves more than teenagers hanging out for a pizza party after a movie. It requires more than perpetual fund-raisers. It looks beyond picking up trash on the highway to get the congregation's name on a road sign. Youth ministry forms an integral part of the congregation's overall ministry in the community. Involving youth before, during, and after confirmation helps them grow as followers of Jesus Christ. Youth ministry validates the congregation's efforts to reach families with the Gospel in meaningful ways. The congregational connection to youth ministry celebrates God's work in our hearts for the salvation of our souls while He prepares us for eternity through our daily lives on earth with one another.

Using the Resource Pages

The resource pages at the end of this chapter help identify the congregational connections for youth ministry within your church. Together with the leaders of your congregation, conduct interviews with church members to gather information about your ministry. As a team, discuss the results and identify the common themes and opportunities God has provided for you to minister to and through the youth of your congregation.

Each worksheet section identifies examples discussed in the chapter. You may need to adapt the questions and survey group according to the needs of your congregation. Do not interview any person more than once.

Step 1: Leading youth and adults into mature discipleship.

The names gathered in this section will identify a pool of people to interview concerning the vision for youth ministry in your congregation. Distribute copies of Resource Page 7A. Instruct participants to complete the statements using the names of individuals they know. They may use names only once. Do not repeat names in different categories.

Step 2: God Himself works to establish relationships with His people.

The answers in this section will identify the ways God could use youth ministry in your congregation to further His kingdom. Using phone or in-person interviews, ask each of the people identified in Step 1 the questions found on Resource Page 7B. Use copies of Resource Page 7B to record answers for later tabulation. Note which answers came from youth and which were from adults. Collect all of the answers and catalog them according to the question. Identify common and opposing themes from youth and adults. Summarize your data, giving priority to answers with more than 50% agreement. Note any major differences between youth and adults.

Step 3: Work to accomplish God's purposes through your congregation.

This section identifies the duties and tasks that leaders of youth ministry could use to build an effective congregational connection to youth ministry. Using the data summary from Step 2, discuss the questions on Resource Page 7C with youth and adult leaders in your congregation.

Summarize the information as ministry descriptions of what God does now and what He invites your congregation to do through youth ministry in the future. Distribute these descriptions to the participants in your meeting and to congregational leaders.

Pray about each of the possible ministries and then select the one(s) that you believe God desires your youth ministry to undertake.

Step 4: God provides resources for youth ministry.

Based on the information identified in Step 3, identify the resources needed for the ministries that God invites you to do for His kingdom's sake. Summarize your answers on Resource Page 7D and distribute to your planning participants and other adult leaders.

Step 5: Leading God's people into a lifetime of discipleship requires direction.

Complete the following questions and use the information you generate in Step 4 to establish your own goals, approaches, boundaries, and evaluation standards for your ministry project.

* *What will youth ministry participants do that will encourage them to grow into a mature faith in Jesus Christ?*

* *How will we intentionally facilitate spiritual growth?*

* *How will we invite those who do not yet know Christ to meet Him?*

* *As we plan the project, what do we need to do for one another as leaders and participants?*

* *When we are not meeting together, what decisions must be made by the leaders?*

Step 6: Youth ministry benefits the whole community.

Use this section to identify ways new youth ministry endeavors support the congregation's overall ministry in the community. Arrange a time to talk to your pastor and other congregation leaders who provide vision for ministry areas. Describe your ministry project to these people and ask the following questions. Share the information you gain with your planning team.

* *What unique aspects of this project will enhance the congregation's ministry goals and reach people for Jesus Christ?*

* *How will this ministry project bring those in the congregation into more mature service?*

* *How can we effectively communicate our ministry plans and results to the congregation?*

Complete the statements using the names of people you know personally. You may use names only once, so put them where they **best** fit. Do not repeat names in different categories. If you need more names, ask others you know to help you complete the exercise.

Name three youth who attend worship at least once a month and three adults who love youth and attend worship at least once a month.

Identify three youth and three adults who participated in two youth ministry activities in the past three months.

Identify three youth and three adults who have participated in one or two youth ministry activities in the past year.

List six youth that you have talked to in the past four months about their personal lives at home, school, work, or extracurricular and community activities.

Identify six adults who have provided leadership to youth at church and/or in the community in a significant way in the past four months.

Which ministries in our congregation give you a sense of personal satisfaction as you seek to accomplish God's purposes?

What activities let you celebrate your faith in Jesus Christ in meaningful ways?

To what programs do you give your personal priority in the church or the community?

What activities do you put on your personal calendar?

What do you think our youth ministry could do to make a significant impact in our congregation or in our community?

What could our youth do that would help them touch the lives of others?

How does God use the people we interviewed for ministry in our congregation and in the community?

What needs, addressed by these individuals, do we address as a congregation through youth ministry?

What additional needs, addressed by these individuals, could we address as a congregation through youth ministry?

Who already benefits from the work of these individuals?

Who could benefit from the work of combined efforts through youth ministry?

Where does God want us to be working now?

What current resources could be used for youth ministry:

People inside the congregation?

People outside the congregation?

Church property?

Church equipment?

Church budget?

Youth-generated funds?

Outside funding?

What additional resources do we need for youth ministry:

People inside the congregation?

People outside the congregation?

Church property?

Church equipment?

Church budget?

Youth-generated funds?

Outside funding?

What spiritual growth could we anticipate in each of these groups:

Youth participants?

Youth leaders and adult counselors?

The people we seek to serve?

Involving Parents (and Other Adults) in Youth Ministry

BY TIM LINDEMAN

Mike's parents were heartbroken. Usually even-tempered, Mike had suddenly developed mood swings that exploded in a volcano of hurtful words four, five, or six times each day. None of their other children had gone through anything like this, and Mike's parents didn't have a clue about what to do. They would scold and try to reason with him. He would promise to do better, but ten minutes later explode again. Mike's parents grounded him, only to have him experience more outbursts. Finally, they approached their pastor with their concerns. What should they do? Was this normal behavior for a teenage boy? Do other parents experience similar concerns?

Too often, parents feel ill-equipped and poorly trained to raise children, much less deal with the challenges that come with adolescence. A strong youth ministry in your congregation can help families like Mike's. How? Consider some of the following:

Regular Bible Study

I believe the church can do nothing better for our youth than to encourage parents to grow in their relationship with our Lord, Jesus Christ. Worship *and* Bible study remain vital for our spiritual lives! By offering a variety of studies at a variety of times each week, congregational leaders make it possible for people to choose a class that fits their schedule and addresses their concerns. Parents need encouragement to spend time in daily prayer, to study God's Word, and to regularly receive the Lord's Supper for the strengthening of their faith. Built up in their faith through the means of grace, parents like Mike's can cope more effectively with the challenges posed by life with an adolescent.

For similar reasons, daily devotional times take on vital importance for families with teenagers. Youth leaders can encourage all families to read God's Word every day. Congregational leaders can also offer resources for purchase, as a gift, or in a lending library. Host regular "devotion promotion" campaigns to equip parents, families, and youths to set aside time for prayer and daily devotions.

Parent Forums

Parents—like all of us—need a listener. Many parents feel all alone in the task of parenting teens. They wonder if their problems and challenges are unique. Gather parents to celebrate good times, share challenges, brainstorm solutions, and support one another. It's a simple idea, but an incredible opportunity to minister to families! Some parents will discover that their teenager is really not as outrageous as they thought. Many will leave with a new parenting idea or two. Most parents will feel encouraged in the interaction. And maybe they'll learn to laugh a little too!

Parent forums also benefit the congregation. The youth leaders, youth board, or other congregational leaders can use the forums as "listening posts." Those responsible for leading youth ministry can learn about the needs of youth and parents, areas of concern, issues youths face, and challenges parents encounter. Possible youth discussion topics, activities, and parent support ideas can grow out of these gatherings.

I know a youth leader who meets every three months with parents from his congregation. He finds it helpful to listen to parents and seek their input. In addition, quarterly meetings provide an opportunity for the youth leader to share the schedule of upcoming events and involve parents in activities. The meetings allow parents to get excited about the plans and then encourage their teens to participate. Most important of all, the youth leader affirms and supports parents in their task of parenting.

Parenting Courses and Events

No one can legally drive a car without training, a test, and a license, but no one prepares parents for parenthood. Youth ministry leaders who recognize the need can find topics that concern parents and offer courses during "user friendly" times. If you advertise extensively and personally encourage parents to enroll, participation will usually increase.

Sometimes special one-time events fit more easily into parents' busy schedules. Consider offering one-session classes. Some congregations build special events like these into their confirmation program, requiring parents to attend two or more of the parent sessions offered. Topics may include any issue or challenge facing parents of teens (e.g., handling media and the Internet, discipline, communication skills, sexual issues, drug education, fostering a respectful home, time management).

Videos, guest speakers, printed curriculums, Internet sites, and other resources can be helpful. If cost is a concern, contact your denomination's regional or national offices. These experts will often make their resource libraries or guest speakers available. Ask about resources that neighboring congregations might loan. Often congregations purchase materials, use them once or twice, and then put them on a shelf.

Careful scheduling of events reduces conflicts. Plan parent sessions during scheduled youth activities. Many parents need to bring their teens to the youth activities anyway. Provide childcare for parents with younger children.

Involving Parents as Youth Ministry Advocates

When young people enter the early teen years, the influence of peers increases. What the peer group does, the individual does. What the peer group likes, the individual likes. Where the peer group goes, the individual goes. The influence of peers often frightens parents. Caring parents pray for positive peer influence.

Can we find comforting news amid this migration toward peers? Studies suggest that although the influence of peers increases throughout the teen years, at no time does it surpass the influence of parents. Teens value their parents' opinions and willingly seek their approval and advice. When words of caution and encouragement from parents are carefully and caringly offered, teens will listen.

When it comes to youth ministry programs in the congregation, parents can serve as wonderful advocates! Your youth program can nurture healthy, positive friendships. The church can serve as a safe haven where a Christ-centered atmosphere, wholesome activities, and constructive relationships grow and blossom.

Brandon's parents wanted him to get involved in the youth program because it had so positively influenced his sister Allison. They asked Brandon to give the youth program his best effort for six months, insisting that he attend Bible class every Sunday and participate in two youth activities each month.

Brandon's parents also approached the youth leader and asked her to contact Brandon to encourage him to participate in a variety of activities. In addition Brandon's parents contacted the parents of his friends. All these parents worked together to encourage their sons to attend the same activities.

Brandon not only became involved in Bible class; he also became a member of the youth choir, attended weekly youth activities, and participated in drama ministry. Brandon's friends got involved too.

By communicating and cooperating, parents can serve as effective advocates for the congregation's youth ministry program. By communicating with parents, youth ministry leaders can gain their support.

Start early!

As you think about ways to involve all the congregation's youth, get the attention of parents and young people right away. Meet with parents of students even before they enter junior high. Begin every year with a youth/parent night to gather input from parents and youths as you plan the calendar. Introduce parents to volunteers they don't know. Meet with small groups of parents to get feedback and communicate information concerning upcoming youth events.

Use every opportunity to communicate as a chance to get parents excited about youth ministry.

Clearly communicate the purpose for youth ministry!

Communicating *how* and *why* things work helps parents understand your goals and persuades them to give youth ministry events priority on their calendars.

I can't think of a single commitment I have made without first knowing why I made it. Parents and teens in your congregation are no different. They want to understand the purpose behind each ministry program they undertake. Does your youth ministry embrace the Great Commission (Matthew 28:19–20)? Does your youth ministry contribute to the vision and mission of the church? Have participants been strengthened in their faith, challenged to witness, trained and given occasion to serve God and others, and provided opportunities to praise and honor their Savior? Then say so! Communicate until you think you've overcommunicated; then communicate some more. Tell why your youth ministry exists and why young people should become involved.

Say it! Say it again! Then say it one more time!

Parents share a common, primary complaint about youth ministry—not knowing about upcoming events or not knowing about them far enough in advance. If you communicate upcoming events by making verbal announcements to the youth, the information you've shared will rarely make it to parents. Your church bulletin may share the latest news, but only with those who pick up the bulletin and read it. You may send youth mailings with all the information about next weekend's retreat, but parents usually don't open mail addressed to their child. The church newsletter, special mailings, phone chain, and Web site all contain information, but parents still seem uninformed. A mentor once told me he believed in the "theory of redundancy." You have to get the word out as often as you can in as many ways as possible.

One helpful tactic: have a consistent schedule. Meet at the same times each month. If high school youth always meet the first and third Sundays of each month and the junior high youth meet the second and fourth Saturday evenings, you create less potential confusion. Consistent scheduling also allows families to mark the dates for events on their calendars well in advance.

Invite parents to visit!

I've often wondered if parents feel left out. Do parents wonder what really happens at youth events? Consider inviting parents to join youth activities to see what goes on. You may want to ask parents to contact you in advance. Too many parents at one activity could prove distracting. Knowing ahead of time who plans to attend also gives you the opportunity to include visitors in the activity you plan.

Schedule youth/parent nights!

Playing together encourages youth and adults to become comfortable with one another. Young people enjoy watching their parents "cut loose," playing teen-oriented games and community builders. Parents grow more comfortable with teens other than their own child(ren). After parents have experienced your relaxed and inviting atmosphere, they will likely find volunteering less intimidating. Keep a calendar of upcoming events handy and invite parents to sign up to help with an activity or two. Discussion questions for your leadership team to consider are found on Resource Page 8A.

Involving Parents in Youth Ministry Programs

No one person can do it all! No person on earth can reach every youth, teach every class, plan every event, or listen to every person. Look at the ministry style of Jesus. He chose others to work with Him in order to carry out His ministry. God calls you to serve His church at this time in history at your location in order to carry out His mission. We are the church together!

You also, like living stones, are being built into a spiritual house to be a holy priesthood. 1 Peter 2:5

The congregation I serve has a stone wall at the front of the sanctuary made of "moss rock" gathered from mountains in the area. Each stone used in the construction of this wall of our church is unique. Each stone has a different color, a different shape, a different size. However, each stone has one thing in common: each one is vitally important in keeping that wall standing. Without each stone firmly set in place, the stability of the church building would be compromised. What a powerful illustration of God's church! We serve as the very building blocks that God has chosen to use in the building of His church. Each person serves an important role—the volunteer youth leader, the professional church worker, parents, other adults, and the young people.

Parents remain a valuable asset to the youth ministry of a congregation. Each brings skills, gifts, and talents that the youth leaders may not possess. Parents not only bring new ideas, but also willingly turn ideas into action. For example, a parent attending a weekend retreat for the first time may suggest a schedule tweak for the next retreat, which will help future events run more smoothly; another parent may suggest Web site ideas for the youth program and offer to help set up and maintain the site.

When involving parents and other adults in youth ministry, be intentional about it! Consider the following as you contemplate how to involve others in your congregation's youth ministry:

Plan ahead!

I can't emphasize this strongly enough—plan ahead!! Planning the youth ministry schedule a year in advance *is not* planning too far ahead. When the plan takes shape in advance, leaders know what to count on. Plans made far enough in advance allow you to secure even the busiest speaker or most popular retreat center. Get the activities, topics, and dates established, printed, and distributed easily.

Consider your needs!

Make a list of the kinds of expertise and leadership skills that will be helpful for the activities that have been scheduled. If you plan a service project, start looking for a carpenter or painter to work with the youth. If you want to schedule a Bible study on prayer in school, ask the school principal to speak to your group about his or her viewpoint. For a session on dating, gather a panel of adults from earlier generations to share their dating experiences. When you plan ahead, you give parents and other adults opportunities to drive for events, participate as retreat leaders, help with projects, serve as a host home for your event, or take part in a panel discussion . . . use your imagination.

Clearly explain your expectations!

When asking parents and other adults for their assistance with a youth activity, make sure to clearly communicate your expectations. Explain the purpose of the event and what will happen. Outline the dates, time frame, duties, budget, and other specifics. Be prepared to answer as many questions as you can when recruiting parents to work with the youth ministry program.

Be sure the commitment is manageable!

Volunteers need to feel reasonably sure they can fulfill a commitment. Show volunteers that the activity commitment has a beginning and an end by stating dates and times clearly. Make sure that the volunteer feels capable of doing what he/she has been asked to do. Assure the volunteer that he/she will not be alone in the task. Be certain to make available any resources, ideas, help, and training time needed for volunteer success.

Make it all worthwhile!

Few things cause more frustration than agreeing to give your time and then feeling that it has been wasted. Help volunteers know you appreciate their time and effort. While making the commitment manageable is important, making it worthwhile is equally important. Give adult volunteers input regarding their tasks. For example, allow parents who volunteer to prepare food for a retreat to help choose the menu and buy the food. Send volunteers prompt thank-you notes.

Final Thoughts to Consider

Carefully select and assign adult volunteers. Teens relate well to people who appear genuine, secure, open, honest, accepting, patient and who possess a sense of humor. Not only will youth be turned off by a person who doesn't "fit" with them, but that volunteer will experience frustration as well. Make sure the adult volunteers fit with the youth, the task, and the commitment.

As you incorporate adult volunteers, take care that the young people maintain ownership of the youth ministry program. After all, you want the youth themselves to develop and practice leadership skills. Involving adult volunteers does not "replace" the youth, but assists them as they grow in their faith walk. (See chapter 13 for more on this topic.) The youth in your church serve not only as the church of tomorrow, but as part of the church of today.

But you are a chosen people, a royal priesthood, a holy nation, a people belonging to God, that you may declare the praises of Him who called you out of darkness and into His wonderful light. 1 Peter 2:9

Resources

Burns, Jim. *The Youth Builder: Today's Resources for Relational Youth Ministry* (Harvest House: 1988).

Christie, Les John. *How to Recruit and Train Volunteer Youth Workers: Reaching More Kids with Less Stress* (Zondervan Publishing House/Youth Specialties: 1992).

Cloud, Henry, and John Townsend. *Boundaries: When to Say Yes, When to Say No to Take Control of Your Life* (Zondervan Publishing House: 1992).

Growing Close: Activities for Building Friendships and Unity in Youth Groups (Group Publishing: 1996).

Huggins, Kevin. *Parenting Adolescents* (Navpress: 1989).

Rice, Wayne. *Junior High Ministry: A Guide to Early Adolescence for Youth Workers* (Zondervan Publishing House/Youth Specialties: 1997).

Sonnenberg, Roger. *Parenting with Purpose* (Concordia Publishing House/Family Films: 1992).

Warden, Michael D. *Small Group Body Builders* (Group Publishing: 1998).

involving parents (and other adults) in youth ministry

List some ways your congregation successfully serves parents in the home.

How can you can listen to parents so as to discover their needs and concerns as parents of teens?

Make a list of ways your congregation can offer support to parents as they minister to their teenage children.

Select two ideas you can start in the coming year. How can you plan and implement these ideas?

What can your congregation do to get parents excited about the youth ministry program in your parish?

What purpose does the youth ministry program at your congregation fulfill? (What do you do and why do you do it?)

How can you communicate that purpose to the parents of your congregation?

Discuss ways you can keep parents informed about what is happening in your youth ministry program.

What message does it send to the youth if parents are not involved in the youth ministry of the congregation?

Why might parents hesitate or refuse to become involved in youth ministry programs?

Make a list of parents (and other adults) who might

* have the temperament, sense of humor, and ability to work with youths.

* possess a skill that they might be able to teach/use in working with youths.

Make a list of needs you have for future youth ministry events, and match some people with the events on your schedule.

planning

Planning for Excellence in Youth Ministry

BY LEE A. BELMAS

"Those who fail to plan, plan to fail." You've heard this saying before and know that it applies in life as well as in ministry. At one time or another we all fall victim to poor planning. Think about that poorly planned vacation or the event that flopped. How about the Bible study you didn't take the time to plan? Poor planning not only costs time, money, and energy (things we don't necessarily have an abundance of), but can cause embarrassment.

Unfortunately, poor planning keeps far too many youth ministry programs from being all that they can be. Some youth leaders or groups limp along without much planning and make youth ministry work—for a while. In a short time, however, it catches up to them. Young people start getting restless, they lose interest, and some stop coming altogether. Then volunteer adult leaders get frustrated and short-tempered. Parents grow irate and volunteers start showing major signs of fatigue. Enough is enough! The leader marches off to the pastor's office to throw in the towel.

Does this sound a bit too familiar to you? If it does, don't throw in your towel—yet! Give good planning a chance.

"Those who plan to plan, plan to succeed!" (That's one of my made-up quotes.) You probably haven't heard this one before, but you know the truth behind this statement. Planning pays dividends. In the long run, a well-planned event costs much less in time and energy than one that's poorly planned. Planning will not only benefit you and your youth group, but your entire congregation.

Who's Involved in Planning?

Planning begins with you and your attitudes as the adult leader. First, you need to convince yourself that good planning will help make your leadership role easier and less frustrating. You also need to believe that good planning will help relieve some of the stresses that come with being a youth leader. When you approach planning knowing its positive effects, everyone benefits.

As leader, you need to initiate the planning process, but the youth themselves need to do the actual planning. They need to serve as the think tank; the ideas need to come from them. Adult leaders need to stand back and practice the fine art of listening.

You can provide guidance, but understand that the youth may not always do what you want them to do. They may fail miserably at times. That's not necessarily a bad thing. Failure can teach many valuable lessons. Failure is good once in a while. That's how we learn.

Teach your youth that leadership means knowing how to plan. Good training in the planning process will benefit your congregation for years to come.

What's Planning's Purpose?

Some youth ministries set their program with an eye toward simply keeping the young people busy, as if keeping them busy will "keep 'em out of trouble." How much better, though, if we focus on the fivefold purposes or functions of the church spelled out in chapter 5, "The Role(s) of the Adult Youth Leader."

<u>Worship</u>: Individuals gather together in Christ's presence to hear the Good News of Jesus Christ, receive His strength in Word and Sacraments, and then respond as they praise God, pray, and sing hymns of praise.

<u>Nurture</u>: The church provides educational opportunities for its members to "grow in grace and in the knowledge of our Lord and Savior Jesus Christ" (2 Peter 3:18). Nurture can include Bible study, topical discussions, devotions, guest speakers, and so forth.

<u>Witness</u>: Members of the body of Christ have the opportunity to learn how to share the Good News of Jesus Christ with one another and with those outside the Christian faith. Jesus gave this Great Commission to His church here on earth! In youth ministry, individual youth can learn how to reach out to other young members of the congregation who do not participate in activities of the church.

<u>Fellowship</u>: Youth enjoy fellowshipping with one another. Fellowship involves spending time together, enjoying one another's company, having fun, and participating in a variety of activities—structured or informal—with friends and fellow believers.

<u>Discipleship</u>: The people of God serve Him in response to His love by reaching

out to others. Motivated by the Gospel, individuals care for people in need. Youth can share time, energy, and expertise. Servant events and mission projects provide great opportunities to serve others.

As you plan, help your youth focus on these five fundamental functions of the church—the foundation on which ministry needs to be built. Ministry activities, intentionally planned with these purposes in mind, will strengthen individuals and help them grow up in Christ.

When Should We Plan?

Plan before the new school year begins, when everyone feels full of energy. Much new programming in the church happens at this time. If that time has passed, do it NOW!

Planning with youth can take as little as two hours or as long as a weekend retreat. Depending on the size of your group, you may complete the planning process that follows in about two hours or less. (See below, "Ten Steps to Planning Excellence for Youth Ministry.")

Where Can We Best Plan?

Ask yourself where you can get the most young people involved in the planning process. If you plan at a regularly scheduled youth meeting, you may miss out on the sense of community that develops while on a retreat. However, in a retreat setting participants tend to get overly tired—minds don't think as clearly, participation can lag, and frustration can set in. A retreat usually also takes more time and money. Keep these trade-offs in mind as you decide what will work best for you and your group.

How Do We Plan?

Work with the K.I.S.S. principle in mind: Keep It Simple, Servant! Keep in mind this little recipe and its helpful ingredients:

* *Trust in God (a lot).*
* *Add prayer, commitment, and a good attitude (a lot).*
* *Mix it all together (with TLC).*
* *Sprinkle a lot of discipline on top of it all (follow through).*
* *Keep on cookin' (move ahead with your plan).*

Ten Steps to Planning Excellence for Youth Ministry

The ten-step process that follows will walk you through an entire year of youth ministry planning with, for, and, most important, *by* the youth:

Step 1: Develop a purpose statement with your youth ministry team/youth board.

Develop your purpose statement before you begin to plan specific events. If you work in youth ministry on your own, develop your personal purpose statement. Keep it simple and focused. A purpose statement should make clear to you and others why your youth ministry exists. It will give you direction and help you keep on track. Your purpose statement will help you evaluate your ministry and choose between important and unimportant activities.

Here are two examples of purpose statements that adult leaders in the congregation's youth ministry might adopt:

✽ *Under the blessing of God, we help youth become followers of Jesus Christ who share Him with their unbelieving friends and serve and honor God each day.*

✽ *Empowered by the Holy Spirit, we develop our teens into contagious Christians who share Jesus with their friends and become servant-leaders.*

Step 2: Lead the youth to develop a youth ministry purpose statement.

Writing a purpose statement with your youth should take about fifteen to twenty minutes. Follow these steps:

Divide into groups of four or fewer. Give the oldest youth in each group the purpose statement sheet. He/she serves as the recorder. (See Resource Page 9A.) Read and explain the instructions. Give groups five minutes to develop their list.

When all the groups have completed their lists, have the recorder from each group share two words or phrases about why they come to youth groups or church. Ask an adult to record their responses on newsprint. When everyone has shared, you should have from ten to twenty items on your list.

Ask everyone to focus on the compiled list. Ask the adult recorder, with input from the youth, to combine words or phrases that say the same thing. For example, *food, pizza,* and *dances* could come under the word *fun.* From the combined list, have youth pick out three key words or phrases that describe why they attend youth group or church.

On another piece of newsprint have a youth or adult write the following words: *The purpose of* (your youth group name or church name) *is to . . .* Start writing a purpose statement using the key words or phrases the group chose. This will serve as a rough draft.

Let the youth edit the draft with your guidance. As suggestions come forward, cross out words and add and rephrase statements. Remind students to avoid anything silly or foolish in the statement. For example:

Trinity Lutheran Youth learn about Jesus, grow in our faith, and have fun with our friends.

The purpose of St. Paul's Youth is to have fun in a loving, Christian way, to meet new friends, and to learn about and strengthen our faith in God.

As Faith Lutheran Youth, we grow spiritually with our friends, tell others about Jesus, and have good Christian fun.

As leader, you should direct youth during this process, remembering that the purpose statement belongs to the group, not you! If your group needs help getting started, ask leading questions like "What purpose do we have while we are here on earth?" or "What does God call us to do as Christians?" When you've crafted a rough draft, write it down. Put it away until the next youth meeting. At that time, review the statement and make any changes. Then adopt the focus statement as a group.

Step 3: Pick out the HOT TOPIC selections for the year.

Give each youth a pen/pencil and a copy of Resource Page 9B, which contains the hot topics list. Feel free to add your own topics or create your own list.

As you read each hot topic on the list, have the youth put a check mark beside the topics that interest them. They may check as many topics as they like. Then have each person go back over the ones they have checked and circle their top five choices. Students should choose topics they would most like to discuss at future meetings.

Collect sheets from everyone and have adult volunteers tabulate them. Note any topic circled more than once. Post each set of choices on its own sheet of newsprint on the wall.

STEP 4: Choose the SPIRITUAL GROWTH topics for the year.

Follow the same basic steps as above using copies of Resource Page 9C.
Collect sheets and have adults tabulate them.

Step 5: Choose the SERVICE IDEA topics for the year.

Complete Resource Page 9D as directed.
Collect sheets and have adults tabulate them.

Step 6: Choose the LIFE SKILLS accent for the year.

Compete the Life Skills topic sheet (Resource Page 9E).
Collect sheets and have adults tabulate them.

Step 7: Choose the FUN ACTIVITIES ideas for the year.

Work together to complete the Fun Activity sheet (Resource Page 9F).
Collect sheets and have the adults tabulate them.

Step 8: Pick out the WORSHIP/WITNESS IDEAS for the year.

Use copies of Resource Page 9G to select the Worship/Witness Ideas.
Collect sheets and have the adults tabulate them.

Step 9: Fill in the calendar with the top vote-getting topics from each category.

Prior to the youth planning meeting, make a calendar for the year using four sheets of newsprint. List three months on each sheet. Mark on the calendar any annual activities (e.g., car wash, Easter breakfast, water park trip, and the like) and other major events (holidays, school events, special activities). Tape the planning calendar to the wall so everyone can see it.

Focus on the tabulated newsprint lists from steps 3–8, one at a time. As you go over the Hot Topics list, add the top vote-getters to the youth calendar. If the group suggested love and dating, for example, someone may suggest discussing that topic in the month of February. If getting good grades is on the list, September may work. You will need enough topics to cover all your meetings. Have an adult volunteer keep a written copy of the results.

Continue through the rest of the lists, one at a time, filling up the calendar as you go. Topics that don't fit should be recorded by the adult leader. You may use some of these topics later.

Ask someone to type up the results of the evening and set a deadline. Make plans to give everyone a copy of the typed results. Don't leave the planning session without a personal copy of the results.

Step 10: Celebrate with your youth and adults.

* *Congratulations on a job well done! Celebrate with food or in another appropriate way.*
* *Start implementing the ideas immediately.*
* *Make a copy of your calendar and post it in a visible place at church.*
* *Present a copy of your youth calendar to your church council.*
* *Have the youth make a poster to display the purpose statement. Post it in a prominent place.*
* *When families with youth visit your church, share the plans with them.*
* *Have the youth read the purpose statement aloud together each time they meet.*
* *Review your personal purpose statement each day. Tape it on your mirror at home.*
* *Evaluate your progress regularly. (See Resource Page 9H.)*
* *Give thanks to God, for He is good.*

Closing Thoughts

While challenging at times, planning makes a lot of sense. It reduces frustration and increases comfort levels for youth and leaders alike. Planning makes your job easier. Planning with youth teaches them the importance of planning at home, church, work, and play. It helps to ready them for leadership roles in the church as adults.

God's richest blessings to you and your youth ministry team as you plan and as you lead!

Purpose Statement

A purpose statement will define your group focus. Well-written purpose statements contain 25 words or less. If someone asks why you go to youth group, your purpose statement will answer their question.

Form groups of four or less. No adults should be in any group. The oldest person in each group will serve as the recorder. Come up with seven to ten reasons to come to youth group. Have the recorder write them down. You have five minutes to complete your list.

1.

2.

3.

4.

5.

6.

7.

8.

9.

10.

Topics

Read through the list of "hot topics" below. Place a check mark by the ones you would like to see discussed in youth group. Write in any topic not listed that interests you. Go over the list and circle your top five choices.

Music	Forgiveness	Grief/Pain	Shame
Anger	Money	Self-esteem	Gangs
Homosexuality	Prejudice	Risk-taking	Dating
AIDS	Suicide	Abortion	Gambling
Parents	Drinking	Stress	Divorce
End Times	Peer Pressure	Careers	Creation
Evolution	Sexual Boundaries	War	Abuse
Apathy	Poverty	Families	Sarcasm
Euthanasia	Non-Christians	Abstinence	Death
Fear	Future	Lust	Materialism
Nuclear War	Pornography	Prayer	Movies
Perfection	Temptation	Tithing	Values
Worldview	Health	Jealousy	Doubt
Eating Disorders	Atheism	Unconditional Love	Loneliness
Handling Loss	Handling Failure	Surviving at School	Depression

Adapted from "Excellence in Youth Ministry" by Lee A. Belmas. Used with permission.

Spiritual Growth Topics

Read through the list of spiritual growth topics below. Place a check mark by the ones that you would like to learn more about in youth group. Write in any topic not listed that interests you.
Go back over the list and circle your top five choices.

Feeding the 5,000	Discipleship	Study on Cults
Other Religions	Angels	Born Again
Compassion	Easter	Christmas
Everlasting Life	Satan/Evil	Fear
Know Why You Believe	Gospel/Good News	Heaven and Hell
Holy Trinity	Grace and Mercy	Repentance
Resurrection	Salvation	The Gospels
Is the Bible True?	Worship	Being a Servant
Books of the Bible	New Testament Books	Bible stories
The Parables	Ten Commandments	Old Testament Books
Prodigal Son	Disciples	Prayer
Does God Exist?	Marriage	

Other _____

Adapted from "Excellence in Youth Ministry" by Lee A. Belmas. Used with permission.

Service Ideas

Put a check mark in front of all of the activities that interest you.
Check as many as you want. Add to the list.
Then go back and circle your top five selections.

_____ Serve in a downtown soup kitchen.

_____ Gather school supplies for low-income families.

_____ Plant trees at a local park.

_____ Teach/help with VBS.

_____ Help senior citizens with shopping.

_____ Make care packages for teenage mothers.

_____ Make Christmas stockings for prisoners and their families.

_____ Help at a local animal shelter.

_____ Be a pen pal with a "missionary kid."

_____ Collect toys for low-income kids.

_____ Help church families move.

_____ Cook a holiday meal for the elderly.

_____ Adopt a highway.

_____ Write or read letters for people at a nursing home
who can no longer read or write.

_____ Go on a national servant event.

_____ Do a spring/fall clean-up for the elderly.

_____ Collect supplies for people in crisis.

_____ Help with a church mailing.

_____ Visit the homebound.

_____ Other_____

_____

Life Skills

Put a check mark in front of all the activities that interest you.
Check as many as you want. Add to the list.
Go back and circle your top five selections.

_____ How to be a good listener

_____ How to make good decisions

_____ How to improve my grades

_____ How to use a checkbook

_____ How to pick a career/university

_____ How to change a flat tire

_____ How to manage my time

_____ How to deal with my parents

_____ How to share my faith

_____ How to study

_____ How to handle anger

_____ How to plan my future

_____ How to say "No"

_____ How to write a resume

_____ How to pray

_____ How to serve others

_____ What's right with movies/videos

_____ Other_____

Adapted from "Excellence in Youth Ministry" by Lee A. Belmas. Used with permission.

Fun Activities

Put a check mark in front of all of the activities that interest you.
Check as many as you want. Add to the list.
Go back and circle your top five selections.

_____ Horseback riding

_____ Bowling

_____ Camping

_____ Go biking

_____ Fishing

_____ Water park

_____ Skiing

_____ Go to a movie

_____ Lock-in

_____ Miniature golf

_____ Build a bonfire

_____ Go hiking

_____ Fly kites

_____ Waterskiing

_____ Play volleyball

_____ Go to the beach

_____ Go to an amusement park

_____ Go out for pizza

_____ Play kick-ball

_____ Go to a concert

_____ Carve snow sculptures

_____ Build a float and enter it in a parade

_____ Go to the zoo

_____ Go to a pro sports game

_____ Have a video night

_____ Other

_____

_____

youth ministry
BASICS

Adapted from "Excellence in Youth Ministry" by Lee A. Belmas. Used with permission.

Worship/Witness Ideas

Put a check mark in front of all of the activities that interest you.
Check as many as you want. Add to the list.
Then go back and circle your top five selections.

_____ Develop a roster of all the youth who are affiliated with
your congregation.

_____ Invite youth personally to activities and worship through
mailings and personal contact.

_____ Follow up on those who have attended youth
group/church and encourage them to come again.

_____ Have "active youth" sponsor "inactive youth" in an effort
to get them to participate/attend church.

_____ Attend a witness workshop.

_____ Invite nonmembers to both church-related and nonchurch
activities.

_____ Encourage school friends to join in church-related events.

_____ Advertise church events in public places like videogame
rooms, school bulletin boards, and the like.

_____ Serve on the worship committee at your church.

_____ Volunteer to help carry out creative worship ideas.

_____ Visit other congregations to learn new worship ideas.

_____ Make banners and other worship decorations.

_____ Write/perform special music for worship.

_____ Write/perform dramas or skits in worship settings.

_____ Greet worshipers as they arrive at church.

_____ Bake the bread used for Communion.

_____ Assist with ushering tasks.

_____ Videotape worship services and share with shut-ins.

_____ Prepare youth-led worship services.

_____ Design a special church bulletin.

_____ Read Scripture lessons.

_____ Other_____

Adapted from "Excellence in Youth Ministry" by Lee A. Belmas. Used with permission.

Youth Ministry Check-Up

Circle the number in each category that best describes how well you feel our youth ministry accomplishes that task. Be honest!

1=Poor   2=Fair   3=Good   4=Great!

1. We get a lot of "good stuff" done at our meetings.

    1   2   3   4

2. Our leaders come to meetings well prepared.

    1   2   3   4

3. Our youth group is warm and friendly.

    1   2   3   4

4. We welcome new youth to our group with open arms.

    1   2   3   4

5. Our Bible studies are challenging.

    1   2   3   4

6. We have a good variety of things to do.

    1   2   3   4

7. We feel free to discuss anything that comes up.

    1   2   3   4

8. We participate in service projects.

    1   2   3   4

9. We are equipped to share our faith with others.

    1   2   3   4

10. We worship regularly at group meetings.

    1   2   3   4

Complete the following sentences.

The thing I enjoy most about our youth group is . . .

The thing I don't like about our group is . . .

If I could change one thing about our group, I would . . .

One question I have is . . .

Other comments:

resource page 9h

youth ministry BASICS

Adapted from "Excellence in Youth Ministry" by Lee A. Belmas. Used with permission.

Building Community One Youth at a Time

BY JEFFREY E. MEINZ

I hate to get dressed up! I only own two suits, one black and one tan. I own two pairs of dress shoes, one pair black and the other tan. I own two dress shirts—both white. Finally, I own only two ties, one with black hues and one with tan hues. Does that make me boring? Am I what you would consider "underdressed"? I pray that the members of our congregation don't notice that I wear the same thing to church every other week. If you haven't guessed it yet, I compare wearing a tie around my neck to having a root canal performed by a first-year dental student without Novocain. I'm more a T-shirt, shorts, and sandals kind of guy.

I last wore a suit, outside of a Sunday morning worship service, at my grand-ma's funeral. For me, funeral homes seem about as uncomfortable as wearing a suit. Imagine me doing both at the same time. There I stood in my black suit, black shoes, and black-hued tie looking at my grandma lying in a light blue casket. Can you imagine my discomfort?

Finally, I could leave. You can imagine my delight when I stepped foot into my own home and could change into my favorite red sweatpants and yellow T-shirt. When I wear this outfit, my wife affectionately calls me a giant Tylenol Gel-Cap. My wife dislikes this outfit, but she's entitled to her opinion. This outfit remains the most comfortable one I own. I've had it for as long as I can remember; it seems a part of my being. My wife respects and honors that. It's my lounging outfit . . . my do-any-thing outfit. I can breathe again with ease; I can move freely. Nothing remotely like that black-colored straitjacket I was wearing earlier in the day.

Have I thoroughly confused you yet? Have you begun looking at the top of the page, re-reading the title of this chapter, wondering how my wardrobe (or lack of one) relates to building community? In my mind, my red sweatpants and yellow T-shirt represent a "type" of community. Allow me to explain. Think about the contrast between a situation that becomes constricting or awkward and one that makes you relaxed and comfortable.

Imagine this situation—you attend a reception where you know very few, if any, people. The group makes small talk as if mining for gold, desperately searching for anything remotely in common. You count the seconds in those deafening moments of silence, begging for someone to whisk you away to someplace more familiar—a place where you can relax. On the other hand, you can also remember a time and a place where you were surrounded with friends or family. Conversation flowed freely, laughter became commonplace. You felt comfortable, relaxed, and carefree. Perhaps this picture helps define community, that sense or aura that you desperately try to build among the youth within your church.

As a person who works with youth on a daily basis, I try to create an environment where the following things are evident:

    ✱ *People can be who God created them to be.*

    ✱ *People behave honestly with one another.*

    ✱ *People feel cared for, loved, and emotionally attached to others.*

For me, these three things occur when I am at home with my wife and son. But I don't experience community with my immediate family members only. Community doesn't occur only when I am at home. I know the blessings of a strong community whether I am with my co-workers in our office, my parents in my childhood home, or my friends at church. Within each of these situations a transformation has occurred, a progression from being an individual in a group to being a part of an important community. You too, no doubt, have experienced this progression.

"Group" Or "Community"?

Have you ever wondered why we call them "youth groups"? What makes a group a group? Not a whole lot! Basically you grab a few people from here and a few people from there, stick them in a room together, and suddenly you have a group, right? You know as well as I do that working with the young people in your church takes much more effort than gathering youth from here and there on a weekly basis and calling it "youth group."

How about calling it "youth community" instead? These words do not roll off the tongue like "youth group" does, but give it some time. Take a look at the word *community*. Do you see the word *unity* within it? A "youth community" could be defined as "a unified body of young believers serving Christ and one another while celebrating what He has done for them by grace."

Or maybe you would like to use the term "youth team" rather than "youth community." I once saw a definition for "team" that sounded good to me: "A community of people committed to a common purpose who choose to cooperate in order to achieve exceptional results." Read that definition again, keeping the young people you serve in mind. I would suggest that if, by the power of the Holy Spirit, you were able to form your youth community into a team that fits this definition, you wouldn't have enough wall space for the "Youth Leader of the Year" awards. Of course, we don't do what we do to win awards. We want to help youth and their families and, in doing so, glorify our Savior. Even so, how wonderfully a "youth team" would fulfill these more transcendent purposes!

Individuals in Community

My wife and I have an analytical friend who frequently claims to be "misunderstood." She will ask questions like "If you had to be a type of tree, what tree would you be and why?" Or my all-time favorite, "If you were a particular hairstyle, which one would you want to be and why?" We frequently chuckle about her questions, but we certainly don't love her any less because of them. She simply wouldn't be the person God has created her to be if she didn't ask these questions. When we spend time with this particular friend, we embrace the opportunity to dig a little deeper into our personal lives and wonder, "If I could be a gallon of ice cream, what flavor would I be?"

Imagine for a moment that this dear friend of mine was not a part of my life's community. Let's say that I met her for the first time on a plane, where we were assigned seats next to each other. She might feel awkward breaking into question after question with a complete stranger. But since she is not a stranger to me—instead, she's a valued part of my life and community—she feels comfortable asking, probing, and entertaining me with her questions. She knows she doesn't have to conform to my standards. She can simply be the person God has made her to be.

I feel compelled to mention that respecting someone's personality differs completely from tolerating someone's sinful lifestyle. Imagine this scene at your next youth night. All evening one teen, Steve, has acted out his bad mood. He's put others down and even scowled at the pastor's wife when she offered him some refreshments. Would you say something like this to him? "You know what? We want you to feel comfortable. We want you to express yourself honestly. So we're going to encourage you to continue to act just as mean as possible to as many people as you can find. In fact, let me introduce you to our new vicar."

Wouldn't you, instead, take Steve aside and find out what's troubling him? Caring for individuals doesn't mean ignoring sin. Instead, we confront sin with God's

Law and share the Gospel message of God's love in Christ Jesus. God made each of us unique. We call that personality. Youth workers need to make certain that while accepting the God-given and unique personality traits of each young person, we do not overlook or excuse sin.

Community and Communication

I feel comfortable with the people with whom I work and do ministry. I happen to fall fairly high up on the company's flow chart and I direct eight other employees. Periodically we gather socially outside our work environment. For example, one evening we loaded up a van and headed downtown for a major league baseball game. As happens so many summer evenings in our area, the night air grew chilly. There I sat without anything to wear besides my beloved T-shirt, shorts, and sandals. A co-worker offered me her extra-large sweatshirt. Someone else asked immediately if the sweatshirt would fit. Jokingly, I replied, "What are you saying? That I'm fat?!?!" Her response surprised me: "That depends on whether you are my boss or my friend tonight." Sometimes being part of a community means being honest with each other, no matter how painful the truth might be.

Think about Steve, the rude youth member I mentioned earlier. Assuming a strong relationship bridge exists between you and him, it would be important to speak lovingly but honestly with him. You might say something like this:

> "Steve, I'm so thankful you have become a part of our community over the past month. I also really value the conversation you and I shared last week during game night. Because I care about you as a fellow child of God, I'd like to be honest with you about an observation I've made."

At this point you can explain your concern about the rude behavior you have observed (if it has, in fact, continued). While confronting sin honestly carries the potential to damage relationships, youth leaders take that risk in the light of God's Word and in concern for both the young person and the community. If all goes well, Steve will appreciate your honesty. By God's grace, His gifts of repentance and faith in the Savior will create change for the better (even if this happens slowly and is punctuated by relapses).

Love, Care, Attachment

Quality conversation deepens community. When you find youth talking about issues beyond the weather and recent movies, chances are good that community is growing. Community builds especially as young people talk about feelings, fears,

building community one youth at a time

family situations, frustrations, and joys. Emotional attachment becomes more likely. This process takes a long time. Don't despair if weeks turn into months. And don't try to force it. Remember Jesus' promise to build His church, and keep praying for patience, wisdom, and true Christian love to grow in your group.

Let me to tell you about Wayne, my hometown barber. Wayne served as my church's volunteer youth leader, and he was my friend. I spent four memorable years in the youth group that Wayne led. Wayne had no training as a professional youth worker; he simply gave us his time, fatherly affection, and a listening ear (not to mention a pretty good flattop). As I think back, I honestly cannot put my finger on any one thing that Wayne did to make the environment so comfortable. I simply know that Wayne invested of himself in our lives. He took us to weekend-long youth conventions, camping trips on his parents' farm, and out for ice cream practically every week. We saw Wayne at the sports events we participated in and the talent shows in which we performed. Wayne gave me the gift of his time. In doing so, he made me feel cared for and loved beyond the circle of my immediate family. His genuine concern made Wayne easy to talk to. I even felt comfortable sharing my emotions with him. I've often told Wayne that I work with youth today on a professional level because of the model he set for me more than a decade ago. I have no doubt others from my youth group feel the same way.

One last thing that I remember about Wayne—he rarely led our devotion or Bible study time. That was our job. I doubt that Wayne's decision to encourage us to lead devotions, prayer, and Bible study happened by accident. Wayne wanted us to have ownership in the creation of community. As a result, many of my friends enjoy leading Bible studies today.

Starting Over

It may seem blindingly obvious to you, but it's worth repeating and remembering that each and every time a new person joins the youth community, the group starts developing community again from scratch. Educational psychologist Bruce Tuckman explains that groups move through five stages of development in the process of growing together into an intact community: *Forming, Storming, Norming, Performing,* and *Adjourning.*

Forming: At this stage individuals gather together to work toward answering the question "Where do I fit in?" People find themselves wondering, "Do I really belong here? Why am I here? How will I be different when I leave this group? How will my presence affect (positively or negatively) the group?" Usually people are polite but somewhat guarded during this phase of group development.

Storming: Plan on frequent feelings of discomfort during the next stage—storming. In the secular world, this stage begins as group members start defining the pecking order. Who leads? Who will follow? How do disagreements get settled? Who makes decisions?

Answering questions like these in a group of sinful human beings can lead to hurt feelings and sinful anger, but it need not. Adult leaders can intervene if necessary to confront sinful words, attitudes, and actions and to help the group understand and live out their baptismal identity. For Christians, the storming stage allows group members to learn the norms by which the team or community will interact.

Norming: During this stage, participants actually settle into the rules (guidelines) and define their individual roles, remembering that no one role is more important than the others. I like to think of teams as chocolate chip cookies. When you look at or taste a chocolate chip cookie, you first notice the chocolate chips. I associate the chips with those people in the community who exhibit extroverted behaviors. They typically offer the first opinion, whether or not anyone asks for it. These people take to the limelight with great ease. I also know that when you make a batch of chocolate chip cookies, you need to add a pinch of baking soda or salt. Without those subtle ingredients, you cannot have the best cookie. Like cookies, communities also need more subtle members in order to thrive. Variety among the members of the team is not only valuable, but vital.

Performing: The rubber meets the road at this stage. Time to take the team and get to work! Don't expect that the team will immediately begin performing with exceptional effectiveness. This, too, takes time.

Adjourning: Youth communities have a limited life span. As young people move to college and beyond, remember to celebrate "ending" events with them.

As you work together to build community in your group, think about Tuckman's five steps. Sit down with the leaders from your group and brainstorm ways to help your group grow as it moves through the five stages. What activities, Bible studies, or resources could assist your efforts? May God richly bless you as you begin this work in His name.

Resources

Growing Close: Activities for Building Friendships and Unity in Youth Groups
   (Group Publishing: 1996).

Rydberg, Denny. *Building Community in Youth Groups* (Group Publishing: 1985).

Youth Group Trust Builders (Group Publishing: 1993).

Warden, Michael D. *Small Group Body Builders* (Group Publishing: 1998).

Outreach/Evangelism

BY DOUG WIDGER

Introduction

Jesus is the Christ who lived a perfect life in our place, died for us, and was resurrected for all the people of the world—so we can have new and everlasting life in Him. But each day the door of opportunity to hear this saving message of Jesus Christ closes for many. And each day the youth you lead come into contact with lost and hopeless kids, young people who need to hear the Gospel message of Jesus Christ. God wants to use His people, even teens, to share His message of hope.

The students in your congregation could serve as conveyers of hope in a dying world. They willingly invest themselves in the ministry of the church, more so than any generation I have seen before. This chapter explores God's activity—how He can and will bring the lost into new life through young people whom He empowers by His Spirit.

God @ Work

Dan and Outreach

Dan was a skinny, uncertain, and quiet 14-year-old. You could see that he struggled, but you weren't sure why. His family had moved several times in the recent past because of economic realities—downsizing and such. Dan had stayed in the same school district and belonged to the same church, but he had lived in lots of different houses. His family remained faithful in worship and strong in commitment. Dan, however, did not seem committed to much; he was just kind of "there." He seemed to move through life not really knowing where he fit, not at school, not at church—not anywhere.

That year we designed the annual spring retreat for two purposes. First, as a fellowship event for bonding, telling stories, sweating, having fun, and staying up late together. The second purpose of the event included outreach and in-reach—we wanted to connect with students from outside the church and with those who, while still members, had detached from the faith community. Dan belonged to this latter group. Several student and adult leaders invited Dan. He said he wasn't interested. The leaders approached Dan's parents. His mom guaranteed that Dan would come.

The retreat began in a burst of energy, but Dan stayed on the fringe. Still, by the time the Saturday night Bible study came around, Dan seemed to listen. In the Sunday morning worship, the pastor said, "Some of you know a lot about God; you're even baptized. But you don't know the Savior personally." The Holy Spirit struck a chord in Dan as he heard his pastor's words. That moment redefined Dan's life. He began to think about what the Scriptures say about Jesus. After that weekend, Dan began to make more regular use of the Sacraments. Little by little, everything changed! Several years later, Dan began to prepare for full-time ministry in the church.

Lyndsy and Evangelism

Lyndsy grew up in an unchurched home. Mom had an Asian background with a Buddhist upbringing. While raised as a Christian, Dad had lapsed into a true C & E (Christmas and Easter) churchgoer. Lyndsy's good friend Elizabeth participated regularly in a local youth ministry program. Elizabeth and Lyndsy had a strong friendship. They talked about homework, guys, shopping, God, and all the other topics that teenage girls talk about. Elizabeth invited Lyndsy to come along to youth ministry events. Afterward, they talked about what they had experienced. Elizabeth prayed regularly for her friend and, as a part of the church youth leadership team, received training in sharing the love of Christ. After several months, Lyndsy started coming to Bible class almost every week. The Holy Spirit was working. Before the year ended, Lyndsy expressed her faith in Jesus as the Savior and asked to be baptized. God used an intentional evangelism plan to create a defining moment for both Lyndsy and Elizabeth.

Caleb and Servanthood

Caleb had a tough home life. Dad suffered from a chronic mental illness and could not keep a job. Mom worked two jobs to provide for three growing sons and care for her husband. As the eldest son, Caleb felt responsible to help the family.

Between football practice, a job of his own, his studies, and family pressures, Caleb experienced frequent depression and anxiety. To relieve some of the emotional pressure, Caleb went out with the team on weekends—usually to drink. Although he occasionally attended church, Caleb did not get involved in the youth ministry.

In August of his junior year, the youth Bible class leader phoned Caleb and invited him to attend. To everyone's surprise—even his own—Caleb came. For the first two months he never said a word, but he kept coming. During December, he began to open up.

Somehow, Caleb's Bible class group heard about his life at home. As Christmas approached, the group decided to pitch in. They secretly bought Caleb and his brothers some clothes for Christmas. The anonymous gifts sealed for Caleb the care he felt in the group. The next summer Caleb attended a weeklong servant camp on an American-Indian reservation. During that experience, Caleb blossomed. Now, as Caleb enters his senior year in high school, the fire kindled by the Holy Spirit still burns brightly.

God used several touch points along Caleb's journey: a caring Bible class leader, the Christian love of Caleb's friends, an extended trip to serve others. At each point, the Word was at work. Eventually, that Word transformed Caleb's life.

The Big Danger!

Many youth leaders hesitate when it comes to the area of outreach/evangelism. The reasons for hesitancy may include a lack of confidence, training, or background. But let's be honest! Our real problem involves unbelief. If we listen to our Savior, we know that a dying, hell-bound world needs to hear the message of His cross and resurrection. Someone I know once said, "Everything we do apart from evangelism is like rearranging the furniture while the house is burning down." *Take a moment and react to this statement.*

Knowing, intellectually, the need, we still often fail to act on it. Why? Do youth differ from their adult leaders in this regard? To answer this question, the Texas District Lutheran Church—Missouri Synod Youth Leadership Team partnered with the Barna Research Group to study teens and their attitudes, beliefs, and actions regarding personal faith sharing. In trying to understand how to best mobilize, equip, and encourage teens to share their faith with their friends, we asked a number of questions about personal evangelism. The survey addressed the barriers that teens face when sharing their faith, how teens feel about sharing their faith, and their participation in personal evangelism. As you review the study, look at the questions and think about the implications for your ministry setting. To talk about this with a group, use copies of Resource Page 11A.

A few facts will help you understand the survey data:

   ✱ *The survey involved a random sampling of 29 congregations.*

* *359 youths responded.*

* *Students surveyed were from all types of congregations—large and small; rural, suburban, and city; professional youth leader and lay leader driven.*

Prayer Outreach/Evangelism

According to the study, one-fifth of Texas District teens (20%) contend that they have identified a <u>few non-Christian friends for whom they pray regularly</u>. Another third (32%) report that the statement describes them "somewhat accurately."

While a sound minority of teens commit themselves to pray privately for their non-Christian friends, the number drops significantly when it comes to <u>praying with their non-Christian friends for them to come to faith in Christ</u>. In total, only 11% said that this idea describes them "very accurately"; 24% reported that it describes them "somewhat."

How might you begin to emphasize prayer for specific lost people with the students in your group? When might you invite your core students to join to pray for their lost friends?

Ways Students Share Faith

Evangelism techniques. According to the study, one out of every ten Texas District LCMS teens (10%) <u>shares their faith in Jesus with their non-Christian friends whenever the opportunity presents itself</u> (registering the statement as a very accurate description of them). An additional 38% said this statement described them "somewhat accurately."

Less than half (48%) of the students said that <u>sharing their faith whenever the opportunity presents itself</u> describes them "accurately" or "somewhat accurately."

How might you help students see opportunities that God creates around them? Could your students talk off-the-cuff for 60 seconds about the benefits of Jesus' presence in their lives?

About one-tenth of Texas LCMS teens (10%) make a <u>habit of inviting their non-Christian friends</u> to youth ministry events—marking the statement as a "very accurate" description of themselves. A full one-fifth (22%) say that the statement describes them "somewhat accurately."

How does your ministry remind youth to invite young people from outside the church to Bible study and other events? Do you host outreach/evangelism events designed to give unbelievers an understanding of Christ's work?

The survey also found that 44% of students strongly agree with the statement that they want their group to <u>host more outreach events</u> and 89% agree that they would like to see their <u>group hold more events where they could bring their non-Christian friends.</u>

Barriers to Evangelism

Concentrating specifically on the perceived barriers to sharing their faith, we constructed a module of questions to determine the top hurdles for teens when it comes to personal witness. In this module, we gave teens a list of eight factors that might keep them from sharing their faith. We asked students to rank the top three. A variety of barriers arise for these teens when they consider whether to talk about Jesus with their non-Christian friends. Here are the most frequent responses (total = 238):

I can't ever seem to find the right time to talk about my faith—48%

I don't feel like I know how to share my faith in Christ with non-Christians—48%

I do not know enough about the Bible to answer their questions—47%

I am nervous about what people will think if I talk about God—42%

Unless my friends ask, I don't feel comfortable talking about my faith—35%

It is hard to tell if someone is a Christian—23%

I don't know what I really believe about God in the first place—7%

It is not my responsibility to tell others about Christ—4%

How might you design "barrier busting" events to equip students in these areas, helping them to overcome their sense of inadequacy in sharing Christ? Whom do you know who possesses a skill that God might use to encourage the students in their witness?

Involvement in Personal Evangelism

While the data suggest that a number of hurdles exist in the minds of teens when thinking about sharing their faith, <u>two-thirds of these teens</u> reported that they have <u>overcome these barriers in the past year and have shared their faith with a non-Christian friend</u>. How did they witness? Here's what our survey said (total = 238):

Invited them to a regular youth group meeting—58%

Invited them to a special event hosted by my youth group—52%

Shared something that God has done in my life—51%

Invited them to attend a weekend worship service with me—45%

Told them about a message that I heard at youth group—38%

Prayed with them—28%

Other—10%

In your youth ministry, which students might be open to sharing the Good News of life with Jesus? How can you affirm and support those students who engage in spiritual conversations with unbelieving friends? How might you develop a youth ministry culture in which the spirit of outreach/evangelism is more the norm instead of an anomaly?

Another Significant Finding

Young people have an interest in learning how to witness! Fifty percent of students in our survey said they "strongly agree" with the statement "I would like to learn more about personal evangelism." Another 41% said they were "interested" in this area. In total, 91% showed interest in personal evangelism!

The "Reaching the Lost" study conducted by the Texas District Youth Leadership Team contains many other interesting findings. If you would like a copy of the complete report, you may download it at www.youthministryexplosion.com.

Some Additional Self-Assessment Questions

The following questions may make you somewhat uncomfortable. But the Holy Spirit may use your answers to help you see ways you might move toward more of an evangelism/outreach focus for your youth ministry. For group discussion, make copies of Resource Page 11B.

When was the last time a teenager was baptized in your church as a result of the outreach of your student ministry program?

Do you have a plan in place to assimilate new Christian youth? How might a student join your congregation? Is this process inviting for teens?

Does your group regularly pray for God to use your youth ministry to increase the population of heaven? Do you plan training and events to facilitate outreach?

How do you communicate the reality of an eternal heaven and hell?

How do you teach young people to have spiritual conversations? How do you challenge them to pray for unbelievers?

Do students see their role in evangelism as simply bringing friends to church and hoping the leader's message will stick? Are your students ready, willing, and able to provide a bold statement of what it means to know Christ personally?

Moving Forward

Your Lord can use your group to reach a lost and hurting world! Perhaps you feel inadequate. If so, you have lots of company. Moses had feelings of inferiority when God called him to lead His people. King David spent his first few years as king on the run. Paul called himself chief of sinners. Still, our Lord found ways to work through sinful human beings then, and He continues to do so today. God's work may not be easy or comfortable. Yet He has given you powerful tools. His Word and His Sacraments work! They accomplish what He sends them out to do. Study that Word! Speak that Word!

You can also pray. Pray for the hearts of others to be transformed through His Word. Pray for God to open hearts to the Gospel message. Pray for wisdom and courage as you lead young people into a lifestyle of witness that will grow and remain into adulthood. Remember, "All things are possible with God" (Mark 10:27).

outreach/evangelism

Basics

As you pray, learn everything you can. Ask other leaders to share effective outreach techniques they have used. Attend outreach seminars or training. Learn from everyone possible. Work with a core group of students to develop a strategy for evangelism/outreach. Talk about ways to fulfill God's purpose to reach, teach, and keep new believers.

Above all, trust God to accomplish His work. "I can do everything through Him who gives me strength" (Philippians 4:13). Wait on God's timing. His Holy Spirit will flood your heart. Your words and actions will come from the One sent by the Father to bring comfort. The disciples hid in fear. They received courage in their risen Lord. Let that eternal Easter hope encourage your heart too!

Stuff Only God Can Do!

This may be the generation through whom God wants to turn the tide. The One who could breathe new life into the dry bones that Ezekiel saw has a plan for our congregations too. God's Spirit is the only one who can create faith in a person's heart. His Word nurtures and encourages the faithful. How exciting to know God would choose us to share our faith with others! Think of the Dans, Lyndsys, and Calebs who can experience the joy of God making them new through your congregation's youth ministry.

Resources

www.oafc.org
The Web site for Ongoing Ambassadors for Christ, an "ongoing" witnessing movement for youth and adults of the LCMS.

www.evangelismtoolbox.com
A monster-sized database of resources to help in sharing faith in Christ.

www.evangecube.com
A simple tool to assist students in personally sharing the story of God's redemptive plan.

It has been said that "everything we do apart from evangelism is like rear-ranging the furniture while the house is burning down." Take a moment and react to this statement.

How might you begin to emphasize prayer for specific lost people with the students in your group?

When might you organize a prayer event for your core students to pray for their lost friends?

How might you help students see the opportunities around them that God creates?

Could your students talk off-the-cuff for 60 seconds about the benefits of Jesus' presence in their lives?

How does your ministry remind youth and equip them to invite young people from outside the church to Bible study and other events?

Do you host outreach/evangelism events designed to give unbelievers an understanding of Christ's work on their behalf?

How might you design "barrier busting" events to equip students in these areas, helping them to overcome their sense of inadequacy in sharing Christ?

Whom do you know who possesses a skill that God might use to encourage the students in their witness?

In your youth ministry, which students might be open to sharing the Good News of life with Jesus?

How can you affirm and support those students who engage in spiritual conversations with unbelieving friends?

How might you develop a youth ministry culture in which the spirit of out-reach/evangelism is more the norm instead of an anomaly?

When was the last time a teenager was baptized in your church as a result of the outreach of your youth ministry program?

Do you have a plan in place as to how to assimilate new Christian youth?

How might a student join your congregation?

Is this a process teens would see as friendly?

Does your group regularly pray for God to use your youth ministry to increase the population of heaven?

What training and events could be held to facilitate outreach?

How do you communicate the reality of an eternal heaven and hell?

How do you teach young people to have spiritual conversations?

How do you challenge students to pray for unbelievers?

Do students see their role in evangelism as simply bringing friends to church and hoping the leader's message will stick?

Are your students ready, willing, and able to provide a bold statement of what it means to know Christ personally?

affirming

12

Affirming Teenagers in Their Journey

BY BOB MCKINNEY

I found them in the greeting card rack of a tiny gift shop. The header for this section had the label "special occasion." The cartoon covers on three cards caught my eye. One, beginning with the words "Dear child," spoke simply and strongly about how deeply the parent cherished the young person in his heart and how he hoped that love would help his child stand alone and be the person he wanted to become. Another cover showed a mommy bending to meet her daughter eye to eye. The message confessed that the mom criticized her daughter because she saw so much of herself in her child. The third card asked questions: "Have we told you lately that you mean the world to us?," "Do you know how proud we are of all the things you do?," "Do you know we feel blessed to have a child like you?"

These were *affirmation* cards, designed to carry a message of care and regard from an adult to a young person. Who wouldn't like to receive such a message from someone important to them?

God shares His message of affirmation with us in His Word. There we learn how the heavenly Father sent us the ultimate affirmation greeting in the person of His Son, Jesus. Through the redeeming work of Christ on the cross at Calvary and His victorious resurrection, we receive the gift of eternal salvation. Through faith, bestowed at our Baptism, God prepares us for daily living. This same faith is regularly affirmed through our participation in the Sacrament of the Altar. As youth leaders we have the opportunity to share with young people the affirmation we receive from God.

I count teenagers as among the most important people in the world. My admiration has to do with all they learn and the speed in which they learn it. The seven years whose names include the word *teen* are a microcosm of the rest of a young person's entire life. All of adult life gets its prototype there . . . decision-making skills, expectations, sexuality, success, consequences, integrity, joy, confidence, faith, competencies, the ability to ask questions, personal power, attitudes about learning and life's purpose. How youth become nurtured, formed, and affirmed by those surrounding them during their teen years remains critical to their successful development as healthy adults.

The home serves as the first arena for adult-youth affirmation. Parents build their children up; they allow them to feel good about themselves; they provide proving grounds, instill confidence, and encourage the giving and receiving of love. Young people also need affirmation and building up in another arena—that of the Christian church.

Certainly teens need guidance, correction, boundaries, and discipline. But even more surely, their fragile egos need solid support along with intentional and expressed love from people they respect. A healthy youth ministry must affirm teenagers—help them know and appreciate who they are, what they can contribute, what they can become, and how much God loves them in Jesus Christ.

Some adults come from homes where love and appreciation were naturally expressed. For them, affirmation flows naturally and easily. Others find that the ability to affirm someone requires acquired skill, fine-tuned by frequent practice. Young people have no desire to spend time with nagging, criticizing adults. They want to invest time with positive, helpful, and caring adults. This chapter will encourage you to think through twelve suggestions about how you can affirm teenagers within the context of congregational youth ministry.

Suggestions for Affirming Teenagers

Listen.

The willingness to listen is perhaps the single most important characteristic of a youth worker. Listen! Listen whenever and wherever kids gather. Speak, but don't dominate their conversations. Remember that when teens gather, although they may let you gather with them, you're on their territory. Don't lecture. Don't press your opinions on them. Don't judge. Listen!

Use these listening opportunities to

* *Get to know your young people better. They will usually respond to non-threatening questions about their life and activities.*

* *Discover their concerns. Log them in your mental notebook. Issues raised in casual conversation can become the subject of a future discussion or Bible study.*

* *Be alert for troubled teens. You can hear the hurt in the voice of a battered teen, frustration in those who discount themselves, and loneliness or despair in those who may think about running away, or worse.*

Use what you hear to help you seek out those hurting ones for special listening and care.

Have a youthful heart.

Don't be afraid to throw a Frisbee, get dirty on a retreat, or take part in a snow-ball fight. You can laugh and crack jokes, but do it in such a way that you and they know that you aren't trying to regain your lost youth by pretending to be a teenager. You serve as an adult with responsibility. And while you don't simply imitate teens in an attempt to become "one of the gang," neither do you let your position of responsibility make you stiff, removed, and unapproachable. Knowing the line between "being playful" and "being an adult" will affirm teens in ways that words cannot.

Remember kids' names.

A person's name distinguishes him or her from all others. Calling a person by name means that you remember him or her. Attaching to that name a mention of something of importance (which you heard through your careful listening) affirms teenagers of their uniqueness and individuality. For some adults, name recognition comes easily. Others require work.

Provide structure.

Structure involves rules and set procedures. Teens will fight it, but they need it—especially junior high students. Kids need to know the rules—both what is acceptable and what will happen next. Knowing the expectations makes teens feel safe. When you go about things in an organized and orderly manner, you communicate that what you do has importance, thereby lending a sense of direction and purpose to what you ask them to do.

Involve them.

Give teens an important piece of the action, but don't just dump the whole task on them. Invite youth to join you in the planning process and in delegating responsibilities. Use planning time to train young people to think in terms of goals, procedures, representation, and involving others. Give teens a sense of ownership and teach them to accept responsibility. The project may not end up the way you envisioned it, but that's fine. It's not your youth group; it's theirs.

Basics

Be flexible.

Flexibility involves the ability to adapt, to make course changes, and to adjust planned events to the people in attendance. Too many youth Bible studies or discussions have gone astray because the leader was inflexible. The printed material says spend 20 minutes in discussion, and spend 20 minutes in discussion we will, whether it connects or not. Teaching teens does not mean making them fit into the subject to be learned. Rather, it looks for "teachable moments," when kids readily listen, process, and learn. A similar need for flexibility exists in all aspects of youth leadership, not just the ministry of teaching.

Understand teens developmentally.

During the teen years, young people change dramatically—physically, emotionally, and psychologically. Knowing what changes happen, when they happen, and the effects of those changes on individuals helps leaders design activities that fit young people. Consider the following developmentally sensitive observations:

* *Never "arm" junior highers with anything that can turn into a projectile. Likewise, avoid games that require middle school students to come in physical contact with one another.*

* *Do not be surprised at the language used by an angry high schooler. But also don't act surprised at the depth of conversation about guilt, faith, and forgiveness you can have while waiting for a senior high student's ride after a youth event.*

Guard and protect their self-esteem.

Do not tolerate verbal attacks on a teenager's self-esteem, either by adults or other teens. However, we need to exercise caution not to overreact in this area. Teens tease one another, sometimes rather harshly. They become masters of the put-down and the sarcastic comment. We want to derail instances where sarcasm may cause serious injury to a teen's self-esteem.

Understand that you work with kids by permission.

Teens *permit* adults to lead them. That factor becomes increasingly important as teens get older. Younger teens need adult counselors to provide avenues of non-parental social interaction. But older teens tend to act cautiously with those whom they let into their lives. Many a well-intentioned youth leader became useless because he or she did not seek or receive the permission of the young people to lead them. Your work among teenagers should involve a ministry of permission and affirmation.

Be yourself.

If one of the goals of youth ministry focuses on helping young people become comfortable with who they are, then they will need to see that quality in the adults who work with them. Teens quickly spot pretense, and it can work against your goals.

If your musical tastes move toward "soft rock—less talk," then don't deny it. If youth know you willingly listen to their music, they will excuse you for yours. In everything, act honestly. If you don't know the answer to the question, say, "I don't know, but I'll find out by next Sunday." Then find out.

Let them see Jesus.

In the end, all the learning, all the youth events, all the talk serves to help young people grow in their faith in Jesus Christ. His message of salvation must remain central to all you do. His love and acceptance should exist as the focus for your acceptance and love for teens. Through the Spirit working in you, they will see and experience the love of God in action. Sometimes even well-meaning adults get caught up so much in program and activity details that the adults actually hinder opportunities for the Lord to touch teenage lives. Let God touch them. Let them see Jesus.

Care for kids.

Sue, age 14, just broke up with Billy, age 15. Sue becomes upset, certain that her dating life is over. You know she will survive to find another boyfriend, but she has serious doubts. So you listen to her, look at her photos, cry with her, talk with her, and share some larger perspectives with her—you care for her.

In a sense, all twelve of these affirmation suggestions serve as variations on the theme of caring. Active caring *is* affirmation. All these things take time. It's easy to operate the youth program like a business. But a ministry to teens that makes a difference puts the needs of the young people before its own while letting them see Jesus. When you stay on task in affirming teens, then you create a ministry that helps them grow into whole and healthy adults who contribute to society while sharing the presence and power of the Savior with others.

Applying These Suggestions to Your Situation

This chapter will prove most helpful to you if you invest some time thinking and talking about it. One way to do that is to gather the youth ministry leaders in your parish to read and talk about these thoughts. Use the following questions to guide your discussions. (For a large group you may wish to make copies of Resource Page 12A.)

Listen.

What kinds of things do you hear when you really listen to kids? When you were a teen, did you talk about similar things? How tempting is it to jump in with an adult correction or opinion? Besides youth ministry, where else in your congregation do youths and adults talk and share interests?

Have a youthful heart.

How can adults in your parish walk the line between being playful and being adult? Name the people who seem really good at that. In what ministry are these people presently involved?

Remember kids' names.

Share an embarrassing moment when you had difficulty remembering someone's name. Within your group, share techniques to assist you in remembering names.

Provide structure.

Think about a past youth activity that seemed in hindsight to have a poorly designed structure. What could have been done better? Recall a youth event that seemed to flow very smoothly. What part did planning and structure have to do with the flow?

Involve them.

In your parish's youth ministry, where are teenagers most involved? Where else might they desire involvement? How could you invite youth to join you in the planning process?

Be flexible.

Why does youth ministry force adults into flexibility? Recall a "teachable moment" that you once experienced. Can you program for such moments?

Understand teens developmentally.

Could you use more study in this area? Whom in your parish or community could you invite to talk with your leaders and parents about the developmental stages of teenagers?

Guard and protect their self-esteem.

Talk about the importance of self-esteem for teens. What serves as the theological base for healthy self-esteem? Discuss, in confidence, one or two kids in your group with healthy self-esteem as well as a kid or two exhibiting poor self-esteem. What can affirming adults do to build up those with poor self-esteem?

Understand that you work with kids by permission.

What implications exist for the realization of this principle?

Be real.

Talk about some of the binds and tensions that adults face as they try to be real with teens.

Let them see Jesus.

Scan across the breadth of ministries in your congregation that touch the lives of kids. In which areas do you clearly see Jesus? Celebrate those. Which areas could use a little Spirit-infused work?

Care for kids.

Use this suggestion to share instances of adult/youth caring that you have witnessed within your parish. Thank God for those people and examples. How could you increase opportunities for mutual, intergenerational caring?

Affirmation Reminders within My Own Home

One of my teenage daughters has a poster hung on the inside of her bedroom door. Neither her mom nor I put it there. She did. It serves as a reminder to show how she would like to be treated or perhaps as a reminder of how she could treat others. The title says, "150 Ways to Show You Care." Some of the poster's listings include the following:

> *#34 Notice when they're absent.*
>
> *#37 Give them space when they need it.*
>
> *#46 Learn what they have to teach.*
>
> *#49 Show up at their concerts, games, events.*
>
> *#52 Apologize when you've done something wrong.*
>
> *#77 Praise more. Criticize less.*
>
> *#93 Believe in them.*

Imagine the affirmation for a teenager on the receiving end of just the occasional application of any of these tenets!

Another reminder, in book form, includes the work done by the Search Institute in researching and articulating forty assets that help build healthy young people. Their theory states that the more assets a teenager has present in his or her life, the more likely that person will be healthy in body, mind, and spirit. One asset is a summation of the book's previous listings: "The young person has an optimistic and positive view of his or her personal future."

Traveling through the seven teenage years is an amazing journey. What a God-given gift it would be for a 20-year-old to emerge into adulthood having been affirmed into a positive view, through God's grace, of his or her personal future.

May it be so.

Resources

Dittmer, Terry, and Mark Sengele, eds. *From the Moment They Were Born: 40 Assets for Growing Christian Teens* (Concordia Publishing House: 2001).

Roehlkepartain, Jolene L. *150 Ways to Show Kids You Care* (Search Institute: 1998).

Listen.

What kinds of things do you hear when you really listen to kids?

When you were a teen, did you talk about similar things?

How tempting is it to jump in with an adult correction or opinion?

Besides youth ministry, where else in your congregation do youth and adults talk and share interests together?

Have a youthful heart.

How can adults in your parish walk the line between being playful and being adult? Name the people who seem really good at that.

In what ministry are these people presently involved?

Remember kids' names.

Share an embarrassing moment when you had difficulty remembering someone's name.

Within your group, share techniques to assist you in remembering names.

Provide structure.

Think about a past youth activity that seemed, in hindsight, to have a poorly designed structure. What could have been done better?

Recall a youth event that seemed to flow very smoothly. What part did planning and structure have to do with the flow?

Involve them.

In your parish's youth ministry, where are teenagers most involved?

Where else might they desire involvement?

How could you invite youth to join you in the planning process?

Be flexible.

Why does youth ministry force adults into flexibility?

Recall a "teachable moment" that you once experienced.

Can you program for such moments?

Understand teens developmentally.

Could you use more study in this area?

Whom in your parish or community could you invite to talk with your leaders and parents about the developmental stages of teenagers?

Guard and protect their self-esteem.

Talk about the importance of self-esteem for teens. What serves as the theological base for healthy self-esteem?

Discuss, in confidence, one or two kids in your group with healthy self-esteem as well as a kid or two exhibiting poor self-esteem.

What can affirming adults do to build up those with poor self-esteem?

Understand that you work with kids by permission.

What implications exist for the realization of this principle?

Be real.

Talk about some of the binds and tensions that adults face as they try to be real with teens.

Let them see Jesus.

Scan across the breadth of ministries in your congregation that touch the lives of kids. In which areas do you clearly see Jesus? Celebrate those.

Which areas could use a little Spirit-infused work?

Care for kids.

Share instances of adult/youth caring that you have witnessed within your parish. Thank God for those people and examples.

How could you increase opportunities for mutual, intergenerational caring?

Let 'em Lead

BY TERRY DITTMER

One not-so-kind youth worker said he thought that the words *teenager* and *leadership* really didn't go together very well. "Youth leadership is really an oxy-moron," he said, drawing a few nervous chuckles from his hearers. "Teenagers are so shallow. All they are worried about is that they look good and who's on the cover of *People* magazine."

The real truth is that nothing could be further from the truth. Across the country, in schools, neighborhoods, cities, and churches, teens take on leadership roles and achieve great things.

Young people have many roles. In the church they live as fellow members of a congregation, fully a part of the body of Christ by virtue of their Baptism in water and God's Word. They witness to their Savior as helpers and friends. In addition, they serve as the future leaders of the church. They will one day fill the role of elder and trustee, woman's league president and pastor, teacher and Sunday school superin-tendent. And while these roles lie beyond tomorrow for them—tomorrow gets closer every day.

For that reason, the focus of effective youth ministry must include nurturing young people as they develop their leadership skills—providing opportunities to lead and giving them something to lead.

As a benefit of these efforts, some very positive things may happen. The Search

117

Institute, in their work with developmental assets for healthy teens, notes that "among the associated positive outcomes of leadership and community service are few behavior problems in school; increased school performance, grades and attendance; increased pro-social and moral reasoning; more positive attitudes toward adults; increased empathy; and great personal and social responsibility."

Think about Youth Leadership in Your Congregation Right Now

For a group setting, provide participants with copies of Resource Page 13A. Think together about these questions:

✳ *Do you think teens in your congregation would say they have opportunities to grow into effective leaders?*

✳ *What places in your church can teens develop their leadership skills?*

✳ *Looking at your congregation and your youth ministry program, how does a young person achieve a leadership position? By election? By volunteering? By selection?*

✳ *All things considered, what leadership styles do the adults who work with kids at your church possess? Do they try to run everything their way? Do they enable, helping youth to discover their leadership style and develop and practice their leadership skills? What things make your adult leadership good, bad, or indifferent?*

✳ *Do you think the "leaders," youth or adults, in your youth program want to lead? Do they ever feel stuck?*

✳ *What motivates the adults in your church to serve as youth workers? Guilt? Martyrdom? A genuine concern for young people?*

✳ *What kinds of things do your youth lead? Where will you find teens doing leadership activities? The list below should get you started. What kinds of things could you add?*

> Vacation Bible school teachers and helpers
> Sunday school helpers
> Church trustees
> Ushers and greeters
> Worship leaders—readers, musicians, choir members
> Acolytes
> Church committee members
> Nursery attendants
> Evangelism callers
> Scout members
> Servant event organizers and participants
> Youth group officers

✳ *How did you decide what was a leadership role?*

One for the Books: A True Story

The young couple attending a youth ministry workshop sat across from the workshop leader at lunch. They complained that their kids just wouldn't do anything at church. "Take the Easter breakfast," the woman said. "We end up doing the whole thing. Like, I knew they wouldn't remember to order the pastry, so I did it. The girls just couldn't seem to get the decorations organized, so at the last minute I had to come up with some centerpieces and was up late Saturday night finishing them."

"The guys are never around when it's time to set up or clean up, so I end up setting up the tables and taking them down pretty much by myself," said the man.

As they ticked off their list of grievances, these young adults were obviously frustrated. They couldn't count on getting their teens to do anything, and it seemed they always ended up doing everything themselves. They strongly felt that if they didn't do it, nothing would get done. The only reason the Easter breakfast succeeded, the only reason the retreat happened, the only reason the meetings of the youth group came off on schedule was because these two adults did it. From previous youth workers, they had learned it always happens this way.

Perhaps this story sounds familiar. Maybe you have had the same experience: seems like your teens just won't follow through on necessary tasks. Perhaps you become frustrated because you seem to have no teen leaders in your youth group. When it comes to leadership, you believe that you work alone.

Sadly, the story of these two counselors rings true. You can figure out why, especially when it's not about you. The couple obviously didn't give their young people much of an opportunity to lead. In fact, by their stated expectations, they programmed their teens to failure. They believed that their youths couldn't or wouldn't follow through, and they got exactly what they expected. Most likely, as their teens failed to perform, the adults got a lot of strokes about what heroes they were for saving the youth events.

An Assumption about Youth Leadership

For young people to develop into effective leaders, they must have opportunities to lead. Adults may offer advice and counsel, but young people can learn to lead only when they have the opportunity to lead.

What Is Leadership?

You may think of the youth group president, the Christian growth chairperson, or the Easter breakfast coordinator as leaders in your youth program. These certainly are leadership roles. Besides a title and a task, what does leadership comprise?

There has been a huge amount of literature written over the last twenty years about the substance of leadership. Any number of books and articles attempt to explain what makes an effective leader. Let's see if we can summarize these as we

let 'em lead

Basics

look at some of the basics of leadership.

Leadership means serving.

Servanthood and leadership may seem like opposites. We have a tendency to think of leaders as polished, up-front kinds of people. They include presidents and politicians, captains of teams, pastors, teachers, and corporate officers. When we think of leaders, we tend to think about leadership positions and may fail to consider the actions that leaders undertake.

The Search Institute's book *An Asset Builder's Guide to Youth Leadership* observes that leadership and serving go hand in hand. "Both involve giving something . . . to benefit others; both require responsibility; and both offer opportunities to learn about yourself and the world. They also both work best when done with compassion and respect for the wants and needs of others."

A true leader serves. Consider Jesus, our ultimate leader. We use words like Lord, Master, Prince, and King to address and describe Him. These words also describe leaders. But when we think about Jesus' leadership style and ministry, we don't think about the cathedral He built or the endowment fund He established and funded. Jesus was a healer, a caretaker. He touched people. He reached out to them. He wasn't afraid to get His hands dirty. He talked with people and counseled them. He went into their homes and ate with them. He lived with them and walked with them. He related to them and defended them. People responded to Him and followed Him.

You don't often think of a president or the king of a country as a server. But in reality that is their job—to serve people. The word *noble* can indicate a royal title. If you see that word attached to a person, you probably think of him or her as of the "ruling class." The original meaning of the word referred to the person with the ultimate responsibility for the well-being of those persons in his or her charge. A true noble shared concern for the health and welfare of the people who lived on his or her estate. True nobles cared about their people. That was the "noble" thing to do. A leader provides the leadership to make life better for the people he or she leads, the people served.

Leadership involves taking responsibility.

Young people have many of the skills and much of the knowledge necessary to make informed decisions and to act responsibly as they carry out a given task. In addition, youth often have an edgy creativity and imagination that aren't limited by thoughts of "we've never done it that way" or "they won't let us do that." Instead they ask, "Why not?"

However, a lot of adults show reluctance in giving teens responsibility. At times teens certainly lapse into irresponsible or even childish behavior (although adults would *never* do such a thing). But often teens don't take responsibility because they haven't had the opportunity to act responsibly. As the saying goes, "You get what you expect." If you don't expect much, that's what you will get.

Taking responsibility means knowing how to think about and plan a task and then see it through to completion. A responsible leader

* *Sets the goal.*

* *Outlines the actions that will accomplish the goal.*

* *Sees to it that those actions are completed.*

* *Assesses what has been accomplished and plans for the future.*

Leadership includes finding help.

Simply stated, the best leaders don't do their job alone! They find people who can help them. They delegate—they share the responsibilities. They trust other people to accomplish a part of the task so the whole task can succeed.

Finding help or delegating is not always easy. Some leaders might not want to share the glory or attention when the job ends. Others might feel that no one else could do the job as well as they themselves. Some see themselves as martyrs, sacrificed on the altar of youth ministry. They want to "do it all" so others will feel sorry for them and admire them for their perspiration and perseverance. They get their strokes at the expense of the teenagers they serve as leaders.

Good leaders know that by involving lots of people, they build ownership in the project at hand. When someone engages in making something a success, they invest themselves and want to see it come to completion. Then it's not just the adult's idea and the adult's success. It becomes a group project that everybody owns and everybody makes successful. Good leaders find helpers who help them lead.

Leadership means work.

A leader doesn't rise to a position and then quit leading, comfortable with the title and the recognition. A leader keeps doing, dreaming, thinking, designing, planning, directing, and working. Leaders don't just give orders and sit back, watching other people taking orders. They stay "in the trenches," getting their hands dirty.

A Baker's Dozen: Ideas for Helping a Young Person Develop Leadership Skills

Teen leadership provides a great opportunity. Teens today have a wealth of great ideas. They possess incredible energy and enthusiasm. Unjaded by experiences and limitations, their insights and ideas remain fresh. With fewer past failures to hold them back, today's teens overflow with optimism. They believe they can and will accomplish great things.

The Search Institute notes that "people become effective leaders through the integration of what they do (the roles they take on, the actions they pursue), what they know (the skills and information they possess) and who they are (their attitudes, beliefs, opinions)." Therefore, youth ministry can do a lot to help teens develop leadership skills and attitudes:

let 'em lead

Basics

1. Provide youth the opportunity to identify their skills.

Surveys provide an effective tool to accomplish this task. Teens can see that God has given them different interests and abilities. If you can, sponsor teens' participation in leadership development workshops, especially those provided by church agencies.

2. Give them the opportunity to lead.

After agreeing on a job, let your young people carry the ball. Encourage them to identify and list the individual tasks needed to complete the project at hand. For example, a spaghetti dinner may require food preparation, set up, clean up, decorations, publicity, tickets, and entertainment. Make a complete list of tasks. Feel free to add to the list as you go along. Make sure to cover any new tasks that come up.

If taking responsibility challenges your teens, break the jobs down to even more specific tasks. For example, "set up" could mean having one person in charge of chairs and one in charge of tables. "Clean up" could mean having one person in charge of garbage bags, one in charge of taking down tables, one in charge of putting chairs away, and one responsible for sweeping the floor.

Ask one person to be in charge—to serve as the leader over each of the tasks that needs doing. The leader takes responsibility to complete his or her assigned task. That means

* *Recruiting help.*

* *Figuring out the best way to accomplish the task.*

* *Reporting on how well things went and offering an evaluation plus suggestions for the future.*

In smaller groups, leaders assigned to one task may have to help with other tasks. Members serve as both leaders and followers.

3. Establish a timetable and follow up.

Help your young leaders develop a schedule that lists the dates by which tasks need to be accomplished. They will know when things need to be done and will expect that you will check on them.

As the responsible adult, make sure you follow up and help each leader accomplish his or her task. Offer support, advice when needed, and encouragement.

4. Encourage and affirm those who lead.

Compliment your leaders as the work gets accomplished. It's always a good idea to offer recognition publicly. Offer suggestions, but not ultimatums, when necessary. Resist the temptation to dive in and do the job for them.

When a young person becomes frustrated and thinks she can't go on, encourage her. Offer ideas. Explore options. Reinforce her self-confidence. Help her see where things have gone well. Cite her past record of successes as a predictor of success this time. Be positive and enthusiastic. Let all your leaders know you appreciate how they accomplish their jobs.

Of course, if a job is not getting done, you will need to find out why. What problems does your leader experience? What kind of help does he need? If he has not gotten cooperation and help from others, try to ascertain why. If he simply does not do the job, what kind of help can you give? Does he need help with time management? Does he simply not understand the task? Encourage your leader to explain the problem. Perhaps by talking it through, he can identify the solution.

5. Help leaders discover the answer to their challenges.

Ask leaders to identify their problems. Make a list in writing. Talk through possible solutions. Let the young person offer ideas before you offer your own. Resist telling him or her either what problems or potential solutions exist.

Give leaders the opportunity to determine their own solutions. Encourage them as they follow through on the solutions they devise, even if you know a more efficient way to accomplish the task. Perhaps, as they try it their way, they will discover another way.

6. Work with them but don't do the work for them.

When you see a young person make what you perceive as a mess of something, you may face temptation to rescue him or her and "do it right"—to simply take over. The youth workers mentioned earlier ordered the pastry themselves rather than helping their teens learn how to do it. It comes as no surprise that the young people didn't know how to do the job. It takes time to work through the details, and it may seem easier just to do it yourself. Ultimately, it is not.

Work beside leaders. Be their helper and mentor. But don't take over. In the case of the adults and the Easter breakfast, they could have invited the food committee over to their house and brainstormed a list of what needed to be done in food preparation. After determining the kinds and amounts of pastry needed, the teen responsible for that part of the breakfast could have placed the order with the bakery while the meeting was going on.

7. Be ready for less than spectacular results.

This is perhaps the hardest lesson for capable, experienced adults to learn. Because they don't have the experience and expertise, young people may turn out a product or program that almost any adult would say he or she could do better. Even so, resist the temptation to "fix it."

* *Encourage young people to stick with the project.*
* *Compliment and affirm as plans progress and when the project concludes.*
* *Point out things that have gone especially well.*
* *Acknowledge potential improvements for the future and make notes for those who serve as leaders the next time.*

let 'em lead

Remember that as young people gain experience, the projects they turn out will improve. The bar rises for succeeding leadership—a benefit of learning by leading. The results get better with each event, to the point that many adult leaders eventually need only to sit back and watch their youth accomplish great things.

Another possible caveat—sometimes the youth will succeed beyond expectations the first time they try. Many youths have natural leadership abilities and intuitively know what needs to be done and how to do it. If you work with such teens, acknowledge their skills, celebrate them, and let them run.

8. They may have to fail.

The teens in the opening story may really have been irresponsible and disinterested in the Easter breakfast. If so, then the breakfast would fail—as it should. Perhaps this sounds harsh. But if the adults run the event and the youth take no responsibility, then it was not really a youth activity anyway and they gained nothing from it. A hard lesson, but sometimes failure teaches best.

Young people don't like to fail any more than adults do. Taking the possibility of failure out of an activity may make the young people's contribution seem unimportant and the activity something they just watch happen. But if failure remains a real possibility, real failure may never happen.

9. Evaluate.

Take time to work with the youth to analyze what happened, what went well, and what needs improvement. Make written notes for the future.

Give all the members of your group the opportunity to discuss the activity. The best observations may come from someone not connected to a specific task. In a sense, these teens might be "neutral" and thus more objective observers.

10. Acknowledge your young leaders.

Tell the congregation how things went and who was in charge. Ask your young people to report regularly to your church council and voters' assembly.

Publicly compliment your young people (and the adults who help). Let the other adults in the congregation know when your young people have accomplished some important things.

11. Plan the next event.

Get started while the memories remain fresh.

12. Remember that there is always a place for ongoing leadership training in your youth ministry program.

Teens will always benefit from practical guidance. Consider involving some of your congregational leaders in the process, people who serve as leaders on the job as they work. When an opportunity for leadership training offers itself, take advantage of that opportunity for both adults and youths.

13. Use youth to train other youth.

One generation of teen leadership can pass on what it has learned to the next generation of teens. Peer-to-peer training can become a marvelous blessing in a congregational youth ministry program. You can lead your teen leaders through the processes in this article, and they in turn can teach these lessons to their peers. You serve as a resource to your teen leaders as they serve as resources for their peers.

Leader Recruitment

Typical youth programs often call for some kind of nomination process, especially for youth group officers. Such "elections" may turn out as popularity contests—the most active or attractive kids become the ones who always get elected.

Consider allowing young people to volunteer for leadership roles. When it is time to select a president, for example, call not only for nominations but also for volunteers who would like consideration. Allow all candidates to make a "campaign speech" so participants can evaluate leadership styles and quality of ideas.

Remember the possibilities of recruitment as well. Tap the shy person who may find it hard to volunteer for a job. Tap the person who speaks critically and always seems to have a "better idea." Let them try their ideas out! You might even want to consider recruiting from the inactive roster. Some teens become inactive simply because they think they have nothing to offer.

Consider the time commitment you ask of people. Rather than electing people to positions for terms that may last for "years," it might be better to ask teens to commit to leadership for a specific, short-term project. A football player may not make a very committed youth group president in the fall but could very effectively head up the servant event once football season concludes.

What about Youth Group Officers?

First, a word about youth groups: for thirty years, youth ministry efforts have tried to stress that youth group does not equal youth ministry and that the best youth ministry programs probably do not focus on a group but rather on attempting to provide a variety of venues for the variety of teen interests. A teen might hate to go to meetings but love to participate in servanting.

With the birth of what experts call the Millennial Generation, we have experienced a renewed interest in joining groups. This new generation will join the groups it values. Churches should look at providing meaningful groups and programs for them and their friends to join. Nurturing this tendency of the Millennial Generation will bode well for the future of church organizations such as ladies' groups, men's clubs, and others.

Youth group organizations usually include some kind of officers. They may serve as elected or volunteer leaders. Youth groups offer the officers the opportunity to learn leadership and organizational skills. Young leaders can learn how to run meetings effectively and efficiently. They have a chance to try different leadership styles and roles. These can help prepare teens for future leadership roles in church and community. The group can serve as a vehicle to nurture some of the more traditional leadership skills.

You Know You've Done a Good Job When . . .

An adult working in youth ministry knows he or she has done a good job when he or she can walk away from a project knowing the young people will follow through effectively. When you encourage teen leadership, great tasks get accomplished and the teens feel successful. The congregation's adult members feel great about the young people who function so well in this part of their church. When this happens, you've achieved your ultimate goal!

The Search Institute notes that adults working to build effective teen leaders "almost always play more of a background role . . . most often in the roles of facilitator, coordinator or coach . . . discerning and encouraging their students' strong points, creativity and independence. It is vitally important for youth to have effective adults to look to. A personal relationship with an adult can provide a young person with a role model, an opportunity to observe and learn new skills and a trustworthy ally and advocate."

Consider This as You Consider How to Nurture Young People as Leaders

For group sessions, provide participants with copies of Resource Page 13B

How do you help teens identify the tasks that need completing? What part do teens play in the whole process?

Do you trust your teens to follow through on tasks? Why or why not? Who owns the problem?

How do you regularly encourage teens to follow through on assignments?

How do you let youth leaders do what they agreed to do? Do you feel a need to change courses or alter plans along the way?

Do you work with youth leaders to help them accomplish a task or do you try to do it *for* them?

Do you publicly acknowledge the successes of your youth leaders?

Are you able to let them receive and accept compliments? This could be *your* biggest compliment—when everybody affirms your teens.

How do you evaluate what has happened?

How do you help your teens discover their leadership gifts?

What leadership style do you have, and where do your leadership skills lie?

What things about your leadership style could get in the way of nurturing effective teen leaders?

What skills do you have that can be used to enhance the leadership abilities of your youth?

Resources

An Asset Builder's Guide to Youth Leadership (Search Institute: 1999).

let 'em lead

Basics

Youth Leadership in Your Congregation

Do you think teens in your congregation would say that they have opportunities to become effective leaders?

In what places in your church can teens develop their leadership skills?

Looking at your congregation and your youth ministry program, how does a young person achieve a leadership position? By election? By volunteering? By selection?

All things considered, what leadership styles do the adults who work with kids at your church possess? Do they try to run everything their way? Do they work as enablers, helping youth discover their leadership skills and style and providing the opportunity to put them into practice?

What characteristics and approaches make your adult leadership good, bad, or indifferent?

Do you think the "leaders," youths or adults, in your youth program want to serve as leaders? Do they ever feel stuck, like this is not somewhere they want to serve? Explain.

What motivates the adults in your church to serve as youth workers? Guilt? Martyrdom? A genuine concern for young people? How do you know?

What kinds of things do your youths lead?

Where will you find teens doing leadership things?
This list should get you started. What kinds of things can you add?

Vacation Bible school teachers and helpers

Sunday school helpers

Church trustees

Ushers and greeters

Worship leaders—readers, musicians, choir members

Acolytes

Church committee members

Nursery attendants

Evangelism callers

Scout members

Servant event organizers and participants

Youth group officers

_____

_____

_____

_____

How did you decide what was a leadership role?

Consider This as You Consider How to Nurture Young People as Leaders

How do you help teens identify the tasks that need to be done?
What part do teens play in the whole process?

Do you trust your teens to follow through on tasks? Why or why not?
Who owns the problem?

How do you regularly encourage teens to follow through on assignments?

How do you let youth leaders do what they've agreed to do?
Do you feel a need to change courses or alter plans along the way?

Do you work with youth leaders to help them accomplish a task
or do you try to do it *for* them?

How do you publicly acknowledge the successes of your youth leaders?

Are you able to let them receive and accept compliments? This could be *your* biggest compliment—when everybody affirms your teens.

How do you evaluate what has happened?

How do you help your teens discover their leadership gifts?

What leadership style do you have, and where do your leadership skills lie?

What things about your leadership style get in the way of nurturing effective teen leaders?

What skills do you have that could enhance the leadership abilities of your youth?

Ministry through Peer Relationships

BY STEVE ARNOLD AND PETER HILLER

Peer Dynamics

Growing up involves a dynamic process of change and growth as the individual journeys from dependence as a child to increasing independence as an adolescent to interdependence as an adult. Each step of the journey toward maturity is significant.

The definition of peers and the role of peers change along the way. In childhood, the family support network really takes on the peer function. The family provides physical, emotional, spiritual, and intellectual support. In adolescence, peers form a transitional support group as the individual moves toward forming a personal identity separate from the family. In adulthood, peers include family, friends, and those in the workplace. Ideally, relationships become one of mutuality and interdependence, allowing for each individual to grow and develop.

For teens, peer relationships become a nearly "life and death" concern because peer relationships become a "family" away from family. These peer relationships provide a safety net for young people taking steps toward freedom. Yet peer relationships can also trap youth in new types of conformity.

All of us experience pressure from peers—pressure to conform and thereby gain acceptance. But teens, unsure of their self worth and seeking a sense of identity as they move out on their own, become exceptionally vulnerable to the attitudes of the significant others who make up their world. A student's perception that he or she lacks acceptance or value can create a barrier preventing that student from learning or growing, even in the best learning environments.

Many things happen during adolescence: bodies grow, minds develop, interests change, and individuals seek their sense of personal identity. This process begins as adolescents realize they are no longer an extension of their families. They must now develop their own place in the world, outside the family structure. Teens recognize that they cannot—indeed, healthy teens will not want to—continue to depend on their parents or their families. This recognition creates insecurity and moves teens to seek acceptance, love, and a foundation for valuing themselves in people other than family members.

Because adolescents rely on their peers to tell them who they are and how they fit in, teen peer groups tend to create complex "marks" of belonging that may seem mystifying, even outrageous, to adults. Teens looking for acceptance in their particular peer group must know what clothing to wear, what words to use, what music to enjoy, and how to react. The challenge for those who work with teens lies not in destroying teen subcultures or in teaching teens to avoid them, but rather in helping teens form peer groups around positive and helpful values as young people grow into adulthood.

Adult Relationships with Teens Are Important

The attention to peer groups and the tendency of teens to look to peers for acceptance—even for guidance—does not mean that adults play unimportant roles. Too often adults abdicate their responsibility and give up on their relationships with young people. Teens may not say it or show it, but they do look to parents and other understanding adults to provide structure, permission, and support during this time of searching. Still, teens' relationships with adults differ in significant ways from the relationship with those same adults and the teens when they were children.

Dealing with young people in the process of growing from childhood to adulthood challenges the wisest adults. How comforting to know we can seek the guidance of the Holy Spirit to strike the delicate balance between directing and getting out of the way, telling and listening, limiting and freeing, shaping and leaving hands off, warning and supporting, confronting and accepting.

Positive Peer Pressure

Popular opinion often frames all peer pressure as a negative influence on teens. Frustrated parents and teachers have blamed peer pressure for everything from poor eating habits to criminal behavior. While it's true that some teens break rules and cause trouble to win peer approval, adults sometimes forget that peer pressure can serve as a positive influence.

Positive peer pressure can lead to the creation of subcultures dominated by values reflective of the teens' Christian faith. This can take place in large groups of Christian young people, in smaller peer groups that emerge out of interpersonal friendships, and in discipleship clusters formed by mixing and combining young people to create an "artificial" yet meaningful climate for growth. This chapter focuses on the development of positive peer relationships in youth ministry. How can youth ministry nurture positive peer influence?

An Environment of Positive Influence

Young people will probably face peer pressure to rebel; but they could also face peer pressure to attend church or Bible class on Sunday morning. Youth ministry that intentionally supports teens and creates positive peer pressure helps them grow to competent and successful adulthood. More importantly, intentional youth ministry can focus on helping teens support one another in living out their baptismal identity.

No one creates positive peer pressure simply by getting young people together and telling them what to do. This approach may work with children, but not with teens. In contrast, when young people help plan and lead youth ministry, it can become an expression of each teen's commitment to Christ and a way for them to be in ministry to one another.

Involving youth in planning and leadership helps create an atmosphere of acceptance. Such youth ministry will more likely reflect the interests of the youth themselves. Teens come into contact with the congregation and find the positive kinds of acceptance and influence that promote spiritual and personal maturity. Young people will not stay where they feel unwanted, but a supportive and caring Christian community fosters positive friendships and gives young people a sense of belonging while they search for identity outside their family structures.

Teens in Ministry to Teens

Oftentimes, those in the best position to minister to troubled teens are other teens. Teens tend to trust one another. They may more willingly share concerns, problems, and fears with one another than with adults. Adults who try to approach some teens, even with good advice, may face rejection. But young people can effectively share the same positive message in normal conversation. Confused teens often talk with friends; they lean on one another in times of crisis. Because of this, teens trained to listen and to share the Good News of Jesus Christ with troubled friends can reach others with the Gospel.

Youth leaders can help the congregation's young people create and maintain a Christian community. In such a community, youth can serve and support one another through times of trouble or crisis. Most often, youth ministry leaders need to model mature Christian relationships and gentle confrontation. Beyond modeling, youth ministry leaders can help young people form positive peer groups and encourage teens to depend on one another and offer guidance and support.

Even an event as simple as a hayride can foster relationships. While the young people may focus on the activity itself, you will want to encourage the development of positive peer relationships. Unfortunately, friendships, even among gregarious youth, don't just happen. You need to create an environment in which young people can encourage one another to trust, become vulnerable, and care for one another.

Making Positive Peer Relationships Happen

Certain skills and approaches allow constructive peer relationships to occur. First, and perhaps most fundamentally, leaders need to prioritize the development of positive peer relationships. Both youth and adult leaders need to commit to this goal. Very simply ask, "How can we develop or encourage a positive, caring community?" Then establish plans that lead toward that goal.

While important for many reasons, large group activities don't necessarily build community. Small groups nurture caring community far more effectively. Activities designed for groups of ten to twelve individuals allow the kinds of personal interaction that build the trust necessary for mutual caring. For example, opportunities to talk about the faith informally and pray together develop a sense of belonging and communicate caring. Small group interaction ought to encourage open discussion of problems and issues in the lives of young people. These discussions will not solve every problem, but small group participants can experience sharing and caring that may be unique in the life of many teens. The Holy Spirit changes young people as they listen to and build up one another with the Word.

The development of a ministry that helps young people care for and serve one another in the name of Jesus Christ involves Christian education. A curriculum for young people must stress opportunities to get into substantial portions of the Holy Scriptures. It should also review the teachings and practices of the Christian faith. In addition, you will want to help young people learn the listening and communication skills that will enable them to minister more effectively to one another.

The ability to listen does not grow automatically. Listening requires an intentional commitment and a certain amount of skill. Young people do not naturally listen well. Like many adults, teens tend to be caught up in their own concerns, more interested in what they will say than what they hear. Yet teens can learn how to listen to one another in a way that increases the opportunity for change and growth.

Young people who learn listening and communication skills often become effective agents of growth among their peers at home and in school. Teens trained to listen don't have to work at establishing a place in the youth subculture, nor must they work for trust and acceptance. They already live in the world of teens. They understand the youth subculture. They have ready access to the lives and hurts of other young people.

Training young people to listen and lead effectively does not mean making them into professional counselors. They do not replace adult counselors. But training young people as peer listeners does have benefits. It gives young people confidence in dealing with peers who are troubled, confused, or suffering with difficult problems. Teens often turn away from friends who hurt simply because they feel helpless when faced with what seems like an insurmountable problem. Rather than offering weak words of sympathy, they would rather not even hear about it. But when teens receive training as listeners, they learn that even the simple act of being there and hearing the hurt of another brings hope and moves the other person closer to a solution. Like adults, teen leaders must rid themselves of the compulsion to "fix" the problem and concentrate instead on sharing with and comforting the troubled friend. Limiting expectations in this way becomes a freeing influence for many teens.

Trained listeners can help a troubled teen see his or her problem more clearly and arrive at the answer that was obvious from the beginning. Many times the difficulty in dealing with problems at home or school lies not so much in finding a solution, but rather in reluctance to move toward the solution. Talking to someone who listens willingly can make the decision to act easier. A teenager who has had an argument with a parent about curfew does not need a professional counselor. A high school peer trained to listen can help by letting that person vent feelings and frustrations. A trained listener knows what kinds of questions to ask, allows the peer to explore feelings, and assists in developing a responsible solution to the problem.

Trained listeners know when to refer a friend with a more serious problem to the proper resource. A teen suffering abuse may require help finding the right place to take that problem. Peer counselors not only listen and encourage, but also steer the seriously hurting teen to the agency or resource person who will offer professional help.

The trained peer leader understands effective friendships and can become a resource for acceptance and caring to those who perceive themselves as unacceptable and friendless. By teaching young people how friends act, we enable them to form constructive friendships that not only benefit those whom they reach with their caring, but also build up their own sense of worth and value as they bring the love of Christ to others. Training will enable young people within the congregation to welcome new people and help them become part of the congregation's ministry.

Training for Christian Witness

With training, young people can also learn to share their faith in nonthreatening ways. A high school student who can share the Gospel in casual conversation can have more impact on other young people than any great preacher. The Good News of God's love in Jesus is often best shared in one-to-one relationships. Teens who share their faith naturally and effectively become God's agents in the lives of others—

teens who may never come into contact with a formal worship service, an evangelism visit, or an attempt to recruit new members in a local congregation.

Positive peer relationships also affect other areas of life together in Christ. Young people can learn to care for one another. They might send greeting cards on special occasions, make hospital visits, or attend one another's school functions. In doing this, they are able to communicate the love of Christ and build patterns of caring that will stay with them throughout life.

In addition, trained young people learn to be sensitive to the feelings and needs of others in a world that specializes in tearing others down and making them feel inferior. Some teens have the idea that you communicate caring by insulting one another. True affirmation grows as young people learn sensitivity toward one another, build one another up, and encourage one another in the Word of God.

Finally, trained young people become a resource for ministry and outreach that benefits the whole congregation. Young people trained in caring skills can mentor other young people. They might visit new high school students in the congregation and help them feel a part of the youth ministry. Trained teens might visit nursing homes and institutions for the mentally or physically handicapped. Peer leaders can become special friends to junior high and elementary students to create an environment of love, support, and acceptance at every level of the congregation's ministry.

Through a carefully thought out program of training, teens can serve one another, build one another up, and spread the Good News of Jesus Christ to other young people who otherwise might never hear it.

Mobilizing Teens to Relational Ministry

Once goals become established, the environment determined, and students trained, the process of developing positive peer relationships may begin. Methods commonly used include the following:

1. Discipleship/Small Groups

Small groups have proven a very effective means for developing deep and profound relationships between youth and adult leaders. These groups can form naturally among friends or among teens assigned to groups. Student groups usually meet two to four times a month around a variety of biblical topics. Group size generally includes no more than twelve students. Students in small groups find it easier to be open about their feelings and beliefs. This size group also encourages the development of stronger and more meaningful relationships with other group members.

2. Projects

Students assigned to work together on projects or tasks develop relationships as they move toward a common goal. A project may be as simple as a thirty-minute task at church or as elaborate as a national servant event. People rally around a common purpose and find fulfillment in accomplishing tasks. Projects demand cooperation, communication, and trust—all essential elements of a healthy relationship.

3. Trips and Events

Trips and events bring people together. Shared experiences and memories created together contribute to ongoing peer relationships. When combined with a servant event or youth gathering, this relationship effect grows even stronger.

4. Community-building Exercises

Youth leaders rely on a wide variety of community-building games and activities. These games initiate friendships by breaking awkward tensions or helping students learn one another's names. Some exercises focus on developing deeper trust and acceptance. Although the games are "manufactured experiences," their results can prove very real.

5. Large-group Opportunities

Many students enjoy activities done in large groups. While it is hard to build meaningful relationships in a large group, adolescents often look for validation from their peers. A large group of teens can signify greater acceptance and desirability. Conversely, nothing gives a more negative impression than when a young person appears at an event and "no one is there."

Large-group events require planning with care and attention to creating positive peer relationships. Students and adults trained for discipleship or peer relationships must become strategically and intentionally involved. They must realize that the event is not an end in and of itself, but rather a means for accomplishing something greater.

Questions for Reflection and Discussion

You may want to discuss these questions with another youth leader, your pastor, or some other parish professional. If you use the questions in a group setting, provide participants with copies of Resource Page 14A.

* How could the natural tendency for teenagers to switch their allegiance from family to peers become a negative influence in their lives? How could it serve as a positive influence?

* What roles can adults play in the formation of positive teen peer relationships?

* How can some of the strengths of adolescents enhance ministry within the Christian community?

* Why are the relational aspects of youth ministry so important?

* In what ways does the development of a caring and supportive community help young people in their search for identity and purpose?

* What steps must a leader take to create a caring and supportive community within a congregation's program for youth ministry?

* How can the development of peer ministry improve relationships between youth? Between youth and adults?

* How does peer ministry relate to the truth that the Holy Spirit has gifted each Christian for service to the body of Christ?

Experiencing It for Yourself

If you are working with a group, provide participants with copies of Resource Page 14B. Time for a trip back into your personal history—consider asking at least two other adults share this experience with you. To more fully appreciate ministry through peer relationships, take a few moments to reflect upon your time in high school. Remember the campus, remember the music, and remember what it was like to be 16 years old.

* Write the names of four best friends in high school.

* Write the names of five adults who were not members of your family who were important to you.

* Recall and write why your friends were best friends and then recall and write what you remember about your significant adults.

* Remember some of the things you worried about in high school. Write what they were. Try to remember with whom you would share these worries. To whom would you turn for help or advice? How did you decide whom to talk to? Whom did you trust to listen?

* You probably discovered that as a teenager you were hesitant to talk with parents and/or authority figures and that often you discussed your concerns with your friends. Perhaps you were one with whom other people talked. Would it have been helpful if you had been taught how to listen more effectively?

Coming back into the present, try to experience a caring community by doing the following:

* Sit in a circle. Have all members of the group share what they like about every other member of the group. Be specific. Call one another by name.

* Share with other members of the group how they help you feel that you are a member of the body of Christ.

* Identify and then share with the group some ways in which people have shown you kindness and how it made you feel.

Think about these statements—true or false:

* If I have a problem, I tend to talk about it with my spouse or a friend rather than go to a professional.

* I tend to stay in groups where I feel cared for and accepted.

* I tend to work harder when people tell me I am doing a good job.

✱ *I tend to like people who listen to me and seem accepting of who I am.*

If you answered true to the above statements, then you have experienced what ministry through peer relationships involves. Even adults function through peer relationships. What proves true for adults is just as true for teens. Take time now to list some ways you can help teens in your church to form a caring, supportive community for ministry to one another.

Resources:

Benson, Peter L., Judy Galbraith, and Pamela Espeland. *What Kids Need to Succeed: Proven, Practical Ways to Raise Good Kids* (Free Spirit Publishing: 1998).

Bickel, Kurt, and Carol Bickel. *Lasting Friendship Skills* (Concordia Publishing House: 1999).

Borgman, Dean. *When Kumbaya Is Not Enough: A Practical Theology for Youth Ministry* (Hendrickson Publishers: 1997).

Erickson, Kenneth A. *The Power of Praise* (Concordia Publishing House: 1984).

Growing Close: Activities for Building Friendships and Unity in Youth Groups (Group Publishing: 1996).

Martinson, Roland D. *Effective Youth Ministry: A Congregational Approach* (Augsburg Publishing House: 1988).

Rice, Wayne, and Clark Chap. *New Directions in Youth Ministry* (Group Publishing: 1998).

Rydberg, Denny. *Youth Group Trust Builders* (Group Publishing: 1993).

Varenhorst, Barbara B. *Real Friends: Becoming the Friend You'd Like to Have* (Harper and Row: 1983).

Training Teenagers for Peer Ministry (Group Publishing: 1988).

How can the natural tendency for teenagers to switch their allegiance from family to peers become a negative influence in their lives? How can it serve as a positive influence?

What roles can adults play in the formation of positive teen peer relationships?

How can some of the strengths of adolescents enhance ministry within the Christian community?

Why are the relational aspects of youth ministry so important?

In what ways does the development of a caring and supportive community help young people in their search for identity and purpose?

What steps must be taken to create a caring and supportive community within a congregation's program for youth ministry?

How can the development of peer ministry improve relationships between youth? Between youth and adults?

How does peer ministry relate to the truth that the Holy Spirit gifts each Christian for service in the body of Christ?

Experiencing It for Yourself

Time for a trip back into your personal history. Take a few moments to reflect upon your time in high school. Remember the campus, remember the music, and remember what it was like to be 16 years old.

Write the names of four best friends in high school.

Write the names of five adults who were not members of your family who were important to you.

Recall and write why some of your acquaintances were best friends and then recall and write what you remember about your significant adults.

Remember some of the things you worried about in high school. Write what they were. Try to remember with whom you would share these worries. To whom would you turn for help or advice? How did you decide whom to talk to? Whom did you trust to listen?

Think about these statements—true or false:

* *If I have a problem, I tend to talk about it with my spouse or a friend rather than go to a professional.*
* *I tend to stay in groups where I feel cared for and accepted.*
* *I tend to work harder when people tell me I am doing a good job.*
* *I tend to like people who listen to me and seem accepting of who I am.*

diversity and inclusivity

15

Diversity and Inclusivity in Youth Ministry

BY MARY CLARK

Alike and Different

So God created man in His own image, in the image of God He created him; male and female He created them. God saw all that He had made, and it was very good. Genesis 1:27, 31

Young children like to tell you when something or someone looks like them. When they wear something red, they enjoy finding someone else also wearing red. They like finding someone who has the same toy they do. Young children also notice differences. Children vocalize the likenesses and differences they notice. "Why is that lady sitting in that wheelchair?" "Why is he wearing that hat?"

Teens spot likenesses and differences too. Notice how many young people wear the same brand of clothing, have the same hairstyle, or sport the same tattoo. Differences exist as well. Not everyone has green hair, purple nails, a leopard cell-phone cover, or dreadlocks! But sometimes differences exclude others. Those who do not wear the popular brand of jeans or the latest gym shoes, those who do not have a good singing voice or athletic ability, find themselves shunned by the "in" crowd. Unfortunately, many young people concentrate more on what they see than on what God sees: "As for those who seemed to be important—whatever they were makes no difference to me; God does not judge by external appearance" (Galatians 2:6).

By design, God made each of us unique—alike in some ways, different in others. What if everybody looked the same—orange skin, blue hair, and purple eyes? Not only would it become boring, but it would prove difficult to tell each other apart. What if everyone could sing like Mariah Carey or Luther Vandross? Why attend concerts or listen to songs on the radio? We would all sound the same. The differences our Lord created make the world more interesting and give each of us ways to excel. In Romans 12:4–6 Paul writes, "Just as each of us has one body with many members, and these members do not all have the same function, so in Christ we who are many form one body, and each member belongs to all the others. We have different gifts, according to the grace given us." God uses our differences to benefit His church.

Melting Pot vs. Salad Bowl

At one time, citizens thought of the United States of America as a "melting pot"—different peoples from many nations and/or ethnic backgrounds who left behind their individual differences and "melted" together in one big pot. Today, more people have come to see the United States as a "salad bowl." This "salad" contains many different "ingredients" (cultures). We are all citizens of the U.S.A., but just as diverse ingredients add wonderful flavors to salad, so the diversity of our people adds to the "flavor" of our nation.

What Kinds of Diversity Are There?

By diversity, we mean the state of being diverse or different. Diversity includes such things as racial, ethnic, physical, religious, gender, age, intelligence, and political differences. You might think of even more aspects of diversity.

To discuss these questions with your youths, use copies of Resource Page 15A: *What do you think when you see . . .*

* Someone of a different race?

* A slow, older person in the line in front of you?

* Someone with a physical deformity?

* Someone who is mentally challenged?

* A person from a different faith tradition than your own?

* A homeless person begging for money?

Many of us have misconceptions about people from cultural backgrounds other than our own. You may even feel fearful because of stereotypes you have heard about. Someone who is older may have physical frailties, but may also be someone's grandma or grandpa. Many people have physical deformities or disabilities. The key to acceptance is genuine empathy, a "feeling with" others in their humanity.

❋ Borrow a wheelchair or crutches and have one or two of your youth walk around for a period of time with another youth group member. Have them try going outside and get in and out of a car or building. Afterward, discuss how they felt when they were on crutches or in a wheelchair and couldn't keep up or how the others felt having to wait for them. Have the youth think about someone who has to get around every day with these aids. Discuss the challenges they face.

❋ Perhaps you can think of some other physical disabilities the youth could simulate (tie one arm to your side and try to eat; blindfold someone and guide them through a room by voice commands only).

❋ Bethesda Ministries has resources you can use to learn about mentally challenged people.

❋ Schedule your youth group to work at a soup kitchen (they need help year-round, not just at holiday times).

❋ Young people can learn about different faith traditions by researching them. Perhaps small groups could research a different religion and report on it for the entire group. Research can provide opportunities to discuss why we believe what we do.

❋ Ask, "Do people of different races or ethnic backgrounds sit together where you eat lunch?" *Talk about your answers. Do the teens in your youth ministry exclude others because they don't know them? Because their background or behavior differs enough to generate uncomfortable feelings? To include someone in your life comfortably means you probably know something about the other person and share something in common.*

❋ How can your youth ministry include someone from a different racial/ethnic background? *Consider developing such a relationship between your youth ministry and one from a church with a different racial or ethnic background. Both groups will likely benefit. If distance makes this kind of sharing impractical, perhaps a pen pal/video exchange could make it possible. Pen pals could draw names out of a hat, and students could write or e-mail each other. Later on, the groups could make arrangements to meet. Each group could make and exchange videos of things popular in their area (e.g., favorite foods, dress, slang terms, songs, singing groups, hangouts, activities, Bible studies, and so forth).*

❋ Try a vacation Bible school swap. One youth group would come to the partner church and help run VBS with the home youth group, then groups would switch so each group would help the other with VBS.

Stereotypes

Unfortunately, because we don't always know many people from outside of our "regular" group, stereotypes easily develop. Use Resource Page 15A to brainstorm and discuss stereotypes (positive or negative) you connect with the following groups: Hispanics/Latinos, African Americans, American Indians, Asian Indians, Arabs, Asians, Eskimos/Pacific Islanders, Biracial, Caucasians, Jews.

Where do these stereotypes come from? Many times stereotypes originate with family and peers. Stereotypes assign characteristics to every member of a group. Common sense would question the likelihood that a stereotype would apply to every person in an entire group. Just repeating a stereotype doesn't make it true.

How could you find out if a stereotype is true or not? If you don't have personal experiences with people in the stereotyped group, then you need information. As I wrote this article, I had to do some research. I thought I knew something about many of the ethnic groups I mentioned earlier but found that there were things I didn't know. I discovered that I could find some information on the Internet just by typing in the ethnic background word.

Has anyone ever made a stereotypical statement about you or your friends? We often react with disgust when we are lumped together in a stereotypical way. For instance:

✳ *"Most Lutherans came from Germany, so they are very uptight."*

✳ *"Anyone who has long nails or hair doesn't care about anything but their own appearance."*

✳ *"People with blond hair aren't very smart."*

✳ *"Hispanic people speak sooooooo fast."*

✳ *"All African Americans have rhythm."*

✳ *"Everyone from the Middle East is a Muslim."*

✳ *"High school students are disrespectful of adults."*

✳ *"All Asian people eat rice."*

Which of these stereotypes might others apply to you? How do you feel about that? How could you convince people that these stereotypes are NOT true of you?

Brainstorm ways your youth group could convince others (even in your own church) that these stereotypes (or others) are not true.

We often get our information about other ethnic groups from the media. Look at the news anchors in your town. From which different ethnic groups do they come? Do women work as anchors—especially older women? Are any news reporters in wheelchairs? How does the emphasis that television news puts on crime stories influence your views of particular ethnic groups? How do TV shows and movies promote ethnic stereotypes? Do any shows or movies use plots that disregard stereotypes? Explain.

Challenge youth to watch different kinds of shows (e.g., sitcoms, soap operas, news programs, talk and reality shows) for one week/month. Note which shows promote stereotypes and which seem to treat individuals with respect. Talk about appropriate ways to respond to the producers of shows that promote negative stereotypes. Do you know anyone who tells a joke at the expense of a group (e.g., blond jokes or ethnic jokes)? Have you done this yourself? How does this behavior reinforce stereotypes?

Can stereotypes ever serve a good or useful purpose? Brainstorm some "good" stereotypes. This example may help your young people get started: "For a child to be a good reader, it is important for him or her to be read to by an adult."

Prejudices

Use copies of Resource Page 15B to facilitate group discussion. How many times have you heard someone say the following?

1. I'm not prejudiced; some of my best friends are_____(fill in the blank).

2. I don't even see color (or a disability) when I look at a person.

3. I work every day with someone who is _____(fill in the blank).

4. I have tolerance for _____(fill in the blank).

5. "You people" are really a lot of fun.

6. I go to the Asian people to get my nails done.

7. Mostly Arabs own 7-Elevens and gas stations.

8. I have a woman manager, and she does as well as a man.

9. Indians live on reservations.

10. Jews control the banking industry and the media.

11. "They" all look alike to me.

Many people who say these things mean well. They have no evil intent. But in reality, each of these statements expresses prejudice. Use the thoughts that follow to guide a discussion of each statement:

1. How do you define "best friends"? Do you invite them to your home? Do you go to their home? Do you hang out with them? Would you date them?

2. If you don't see color when you look at a person, then you miss an important part of who the person is. You miss her life experiences. If we ignore her color and how beautifully God has created each person, we aren't seeing the whole picture.

3. Just because you work with someone every day doesn't mean that you develop a friendship with him or that you don't carry a prejudice in your mind toward him. Do you know where he lives? Have you been there? Has he been to where you live? Do you eat lunch with him? Do you know anything about his life? If the answers are no, you probably only hold an acquaintance with this person.

4. Having tolerance for someone can mean that you respect differences, but it can also mean (and in many cases does mean) that you only "tolerate" them rather than care about them with Jesus' love. While we are not to tolerate sin, God calls us to respect the differences He has created. "For everything God created is good" (1 Timothy 4:4a).

5. The phrase "you people" insults people of color. While the person who made

the statement meant it to be a compliment, it isn't taken as such.

6. Many nail salons could be owned and operated by Asians, but not all Asians are Chinese. In fact, "Asian" describes people from a number of ethnic groups, including native-born Americans. Do you know anything about the people who own and operate the services you use? If you ask polite questions in an interested way, you may open discussion with people from backgrounds different from your own.

7. It may be true that many convenience stores/gas stations are owned and operated by Arabs. How many different Arab groups exist? Can you name any? The term *Arab* can describe people whose native language is Arabic and who regard Arab culture as their own, but "Arabs" are not a single ethnic group. Approximately 19 countries in the Middle East and northern Africa make up the Arab world, a region 1.5 times the size of the United States.

Many people from certain regions in the Middle East, including parts of Lebanon, Iraq (Chaldeans), Jordan, Sudan, and Syria, have Christian populations. Many African nations have more Christians than the U.S.; in fact, Ethiopia has a huge Lutheran population!

8. Do you have a female manager/supervisor? Do you or others explain to anyone that she can do the job as well as a man? What if she gets emotional or even cries? Do you think (even for a moment) that if she were a man, she wouldn't cry?

Talk about how guys sometimes keep their feelings in and girls show their feelings more readily. How could each behavior be an advantage or a disadvantage at work?

9. Some American Indians do live on reservations, but many also live in cities and in rural areas across the country. There are many different American Indian tribes. Research them on the Internet or at the library. Or contact the task force listed under the Board for Mission Services of the LCMS in the resources section at the end of this chapter.

10. Many Jewish people do work in the banking industry and the media. Does this mean they control them? The term *Jewish* can refer to both a race and a religion. For some individuals it is both. Many resources exist for learning about the Jewish religion. Many Jewish holidays/celebrations come from the Old Testament. You can read the background of the festival of Purim in the book of Esther (see especially Esther 9).

11. Police training has indicated that eyewitnesses can seldom differentiate between people of ethnic backgrounds other than their own. This "eyewitness" deficiency can occur even between people of the same ethnic background.

Without announcing it beforehand, have someone unknown to the group walk through the room while the youth group is having a meeting. Stop the meeting and have each person write down a description of the person who walked through. Then have the person come back so you can see if the descriptions were accurate.

Inclusivity

To include someone means to take that person in or consider that person a part or member of your group. How do we include others? Why would we want to? The evangelist Luke writes, "But the Pharisees and the teachers of the law muttered, 'This man welcomes sinners and eats with them.'" The religious leaders were aghast that Jesus would associate with the worst of sinners and even enjoy the fellowship of a meal with them. Of course, the opinions of the religious leaders did not matter to Jesus. He had come to seek and save the lost. He made friends with sinners; He actually *touched* lepers—an act that made Him ceremonially unclean. Our Lord simply ignored social convention and religious tradition when these got in the way of His saving purposes.

Are there some people with whom Christians today refuse to associate? Where do these taboos come from? What about Middle Eastern people? What about someone who practices Hinduism or Buddhism? Would Jesus associate with Muslims? How do we know? By including these individuals, Christians have the opportunity to witness the truth of the Gospel to those who do not believe in Christ as Savior. When does inclusion cross the line into manipulation?

Many people are "included" in the workplace or even the church. For instance, a woman may be in upper management at a company or all youth over 16 may automatically belong to the voter's assembly at church. When is inclusion genuine? When is inclusion phony? Talk with students about how they could work to overcome less-than-genuine attitudes and behaviors.

Holidays and Celebrations

One way to celebrate diversity and inclusivity is to understand some of the special holidays and celebrations in which different groups participate. Besides federal holidays, what holidays do you know something about? Write them down. Were any of these on your list?

Ramadan: The month on the Islamic lunar calendar during which Muslims abstain from food, drink, and other sensual pleasures from the break of dawn to sunset. The fast encourages learning discipline, self-restraint, and generosity while obeying Allah's commandments. Fasting is one of the "five pillars" of Islam. Every sane and able adult Muslim must fast during Ramadan. Muslims who have begun puberty are considered adults; therefore, high school students are expected to participate.

Think of the physical and social ramifications that the fast has on someone in the workplace. How would it affect someone trying to participate in class or do homework before breaking the fast at sunset?

Cinco de Mayo: Literally translated from Spanish, these words mean the "Fifth of May." Many celebrate this day as Mexico's Independence Day. Cinco de Mayo celebrates a Mexican victory (named *La Batalla de Puebla*) over the army of Napoleon III. Despite tremendous odds, the humble Mexican Army defeated one of the most powerful fighting units in the world at that time. The victory gave the Mexican people a sense of pride and patriotism that they had never before enjoyed. Interestingly, *Cinco de Mayo* isn't celebrated in Mexico to the same extent as in the United States. *El 16 de Setiembre* (the actual Mexican Independence Day) is seen as the more important holiday.

Rosh Hashanah: Rosh Hashanah literally means the "head of the year" and commemorates the anniversary of the creation of the world. Often Rosh Hashanah is referred to as the Jewish New Year, but the Hebrew month of Nissan—the month in which Passover is celebrated—is the first month of the Jewish calendar. The command to observe Rosh Hashanah comes from the Torah, the five books of Moses: "On the first day of the seventh month, you are to have a day of rest, a sacred assembly commemorated with trumpet blasts. Do no regular work, but present an offering made to the Lord by fire" (Leviticus 23:24–25).

Yom Kippur: Yom Kippur, the Sabbath of Sabbaths, or Day of Atonement, is observed on the tenth day of the Hebrew month of Tishri (September or early October in the secular calendar). In Leviticus 16:29–31 Moses commands, "This is to be a lasting ordinance for you: On the tenth day of the seventh month you must deny yourselves and not do any work—whether native-born or an alien living among you—because on this day atonement will be made for you, to cleanse you. Then, before the Lord, you will be clean from all your sins. It is a Sabbath of rest, and you must deny yourselves; it is a lasting ordinance." Moses commanded this day when he returned from his trip to Mt. Sinai to get the tablets of the Ten Commandments. Moses saw that the nation had truly repented for their sins of idolatry and announced to them God's forgiveness.

Passover: Passover celebrates Israel's exodus from Egypt and is *the* pivotal event in Jewish history. It is sometimes called the Feast of Freedom. The story of Passover is found in Exodus 12 and 13.

Hanukah: Hanukah, the Hebrew word meaning "dedication," is celebrated for eight days during the Hebrew month of Kislev, which usually occurs in mid to late December. It recalls the Israeli struggle for religious freedom and commemorates a victory of the Jews over the Syrians. This victory is not found in the Torah, but rather in the Apocrypha (an appendix to the Bible used by Roman Catholics, some Jews, and others).

Kwanzaa: Kwanzaa is an African-American holiday based on the festival of the harvest of the first crops. It begins on December 26 and lasts for seven days. Each day has a name and principle based on black culture. These include 1. *Umoja* (unity), 2. *Kujichagulia* (self-determination), 3. *Ujima* (collective work and responsibility), 4.

Ujamaa (cooperative economics), 5. *Nia* (purpose), 6. *Kuumba* (creativity), and 7. *Imani* (faith). Each evening, family members light one of the seven candles in a *kinara* (candle holder) and discuss the principle for the day. Many families exchange gifts, some of which are homemade. A feast called *karamu* occurs near the end of the holiday.

Canadian Thanksgiving: The Thanksgiving holiday in Canada is celebrated on the second Monday in October (the day the U.S. celebrates Columbus Day).

Final Thoughts

The census bureau has indicated that Caucasians will soon become a minority in this country. What implication does this have for your youth ministry? How will this fact influence future national leaders? Church leaders?

John 3:16 says, "For God so loved the world that He gave His one and only Son, that whoever believes in Him shall not perish but have eternal life." God's gift of salvation is freely given to everyone who believes, not just to those "like us." As our world changes, we must work to include the people of all nations in the fellowship of true believers.

More Ideas for Honoring Diversity

Many ideas were provided throughout this chapter; here are a few more:

1. Visit places or take part in events that tell about a different culture (e.g., a powwow, a Holocaust center, a homeless shelter, a school for the handicapped, or an African-American museum). Talk to the people who work there.

2. Inform yourself about different ethnic groups. Use the resources listed in the resources section. Find some resources of your own.

3. Brainstorm about ways your youth ministry could become more inclusive and respectful of diversity.

RESOURCES FOR FURTHER GROWTH

Lucero, Maria Guajardo. *The Spirit of Culture* (Assets for Colorado Youth: 2000).

Nunes, John. *Voices from the City: Issues and Images in Urban Preaching* (Concordia Publishing House: 1999).

POBLO (People of the Book Lutheran Outreach); e-mail: pobloffice@aol.com

Rochester, Nikki. *Harvest Waiting: Reaching Out to the African-Americans* (Concordia Publishing House: 1995).

Roehlkepartain, Eugene C. *Building Assets in Congregations: A Practical Guide for Helping Youth Grow Up Healthy* (Search Institute: 1998).

Roehlkepartain, Jolene L., and Eugene C. Roehlkepartain. *Prescription for a Healthy Church: Ministry Ideas to Nurture Whole People* (Group Publishing: 2000).

www.icofa.com
   Council on American-Islamic Relations

www.lcms.org
   Board for Black Ministry Services—LCMS and Committees and Task Forces of the Board for Mission Services—LCMS

What Kinds of Diversity Are There?

1. What do you think when you see someone of a different race? An older person who is slow in the line in front of you? Someone with a physical deformity? Someone who is mentally challenged? A person who believes in a different faith tradition than your own? A homeless person begging for money?

2. Do people of different races or ethnic backgrounds sit together where you eat lunch? Why or why not?

3. How can your youth ministry include people of different racial/ethnic backgrounds?

Stereotypes

What common stereotypes have you heard to describe the following groups of people?

Hispanics/Latinos:

African Americans:

American Indians:

Asian Indians:

Arabs:

Asians:

Eskimos/Pacific Islanders:

Biracial:

Caucasians:

Jews:

1. *Where did these stereotypes come from?*

2. *How could you find out if a stereotype were true or not?*

3. *Has anyone ever made a stereotypical statement about you or your friends?*

4 *How do these stereotypical statements make you feel?*

"Most Lutherans came from Germany, so they are very uptight."

"Anyone who has long nails or hair doesn't care about anything but their appearance."

"That person has blond hair; she must not be very smart."

"Hispanic people speak sooooooo fast."

"All African Americans have rhythm."

"Everyone from the Middle East shares the Muslim religion."

"High school students are disrespectful to adults."

"All Asian people eat rice."

5. *How can we convince people that their stereotypes need to be examined?*

6. *We often get our information about people of other ethnic groups from the media. Look at the news anchors in your town. What ethnic groups are represented? Do women serve as anchors, especially older women? Do any reporters work from a wheelchair? How does the way your local stations report the news about crime influence the ways you see particular ethnic groups?*

7. *What TV shows and movies stereotype individuals from particular ethnic groups? Do any shows or movies help break stereotypes?*

8. *Can stereotypes ever serve a good or useful purpose?*

Prejudices

How many times have you heard someone say the following?

I'm not prejudiced; some of my best friends are _____(fill in the blank).

I don't even see color (or a disability) when I look at a person.

I work every day with someone who is _____(fill in the blank).

I have tolerance for _____(fill in the blank).

"You people" are really a lot of fun.

I go to the Asian people to get my nails done.

Mostly Arabs own 7-Elevens and gas stations.

My manager is a woman, and she does as well as a man.

Indians live on reservations.

Jews control the banking industry and the media.

"They" all look alike to me.

Do any of the statements above indicate that someone indeed is free of prejudice?

Holidays and Celebrations

Besides federal holidays, what holidays do you know something about? Write them below.

diversity and inclusivity in youth ministry

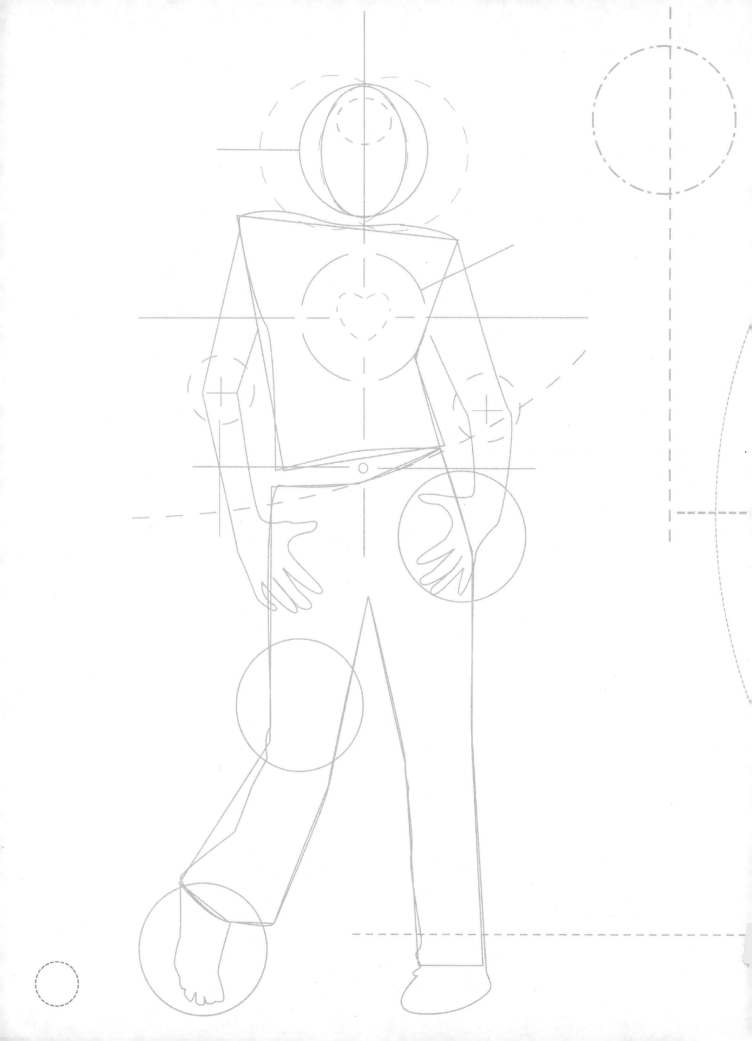

BASICS